S0-ADQ-535

THE WAR WITHIN YOU

OVERCOMING THE OBSTACLES TO GODLY CHARACTER

THE WAR WITHIN YOU

OVERCOMING THE OBSTACLES TO GODLY CHARACTER

DOUG McINTOSH

MOODY PRESS

CHICAGO

2001 by
DOUG MCINTOSH

All rights reserved. No part of this book may be reproduced in any form without permission in writing from the publisher, except in the case of brief quotations embodied in critical articles or reviews.

All Scripture quotations, unless otherwise indicated, are taken from the *New King James Version.* Copyright © 1982 by Thomas Nelson, Inc. Used by permission. All rights reserved.

Scripture quotations marked NIV are taken from the *Holy Bible, New International Version®.* NIV®. Copyright © 1973, 1978, 1984 by International Bible Society. Used by permission of Zondervan Publishing House. All rights reserved.

Scripture quotations marked NASB are taken from the *New American Standard Bible®,* © Copyright The Lockman Foundation 1960, 1962, 1963, 1968, 1971, 1972, 1973, 1975, 1977, 1995. Used by permission.

Library of Congress Cataloging-in-Publication Data

McIntosh, Doug.
    The war within you : overcoming the obstacles to godly character / Doug McIntosh.
        p. cm.
    Includes bibliographical references.
    ISBN 0-8024-6649-4
    1. Christian life. I. Title

BV4501.3 .M38 2001
248.4--dc21

                                                                                    00-066987

1 3 5 7 9 10 8 6 4 2

Printed in the United States of America

To present and former members of the
Eastern Congo Group of Wycliffe Bible Translators,
warriors in the right battles:

Louise Anderson
Mary Anne Augustin
Jill Brace
Shawn and Candace Brandt
John and Elsie Bush
Chuck and Diane DeVries
Fred and Claertje Frieke
Bettina Gottschlich
Jon and Cindi Hampshire
Stew and Jo Johnson
Chris and Donna Langston
Rob and Carol McKee
Keith and Lori Miller
Jim and Jill Pinkerton
Tim and Liz Raymond
Paul and Kathy Schmidt
Roger and Karen Van Otterloo
John and Marian VanderMeer
Doug and Lori Wright

CONTENTS

FOREWORD

When Doug McIntosh asked me to write the foreword for his new book *The War Within You,* I was delighted to do so for a number of reasons. First, I have Doug to thank for the unique seminary training I received at Dallas Seminary. Doug was one of my professors at Carver Bible College in Atlanta where I did my undergrad work. Observing my passion for learning the Scriptures he challenged me to continue my biblical training by applying to Dallas Seminary. He even put up the application fee. I was admitted as the third African American and had the honor of becoming the first to earn a doctorate. The rest is history. Thanks Doug!

A second reason why I am honored to foreword this work is because of the profound impact his previous work had on my life. In his book *Life's Greatest Journey* he reminded me afresh that I am to look at my life from the perspective of a pilgrim and not a permanent resident. He helped refocus my type "A" ministry driven personality in the right direction. Thanks again, Doug!

A third reason that I am honored to foreword this book is because it is one of the best, most effective, spiritually illuminating works on victorious Christian living I have ever read. In this book Doug clearly defines the spiritual battle in which all believers are engaged. He balances biblical instruction with spiritual encouragement in a most unique way. Set against the backdrop of warfare, Doug confronts us with the realities of Christian life often glossed over today in the contemporary era of compromising Christianity. Doug defines the Christian life of discipleship for what it really is, a life of denial, not indulgence. This work makes the concept of settling for drive-thru Christianity (Mac-Christianity) totally unacceptable. I found my own soul getting somewhat ill at ease as I reviewed the manuscript. Thanks a lot, Doug!

A fourth reason I delight in this opportunity is because, as a pastor, Doug recognizes that people don't only need teaching, they also need hope. Without compromising one iota of God's truth, Doug's shepherd heart gives the reader hope. He not only condemns us for not meeting God's high and holy standard, he also helps us get there. When you finish reading this book you will know all is not lost and that God's marvelous grace can take you from where you are to where God wants you to be. Thanks a bunch, Doug!

If you are serious about your Christian walk, if you desire to experience authentic Christianity and the true life experience that only comes from the inside-out, then this book is for you. It will open you up to experience God at the deepest spiritual level possible.

After you have completed your reading of *The War Within You* and its impact is fully felt in your life, I am confident that you will join me in a resounding "Can't thank you enough, Doug!"

TONY EVANS
Pastor and Author

ACKNOWLEDGMENTS

This book became a reality through the participation of many people. Thanks are due to Jim Bell of Moody Press for his continuing encouragement; to Karen Hutto for reading portions of the manuscript and for her useful suggestions; and to Moody's Cheryl Dunlop for her capable editorial assistance. My gratitude also extends to my congregation, Cornerstone Bible Church of Lilburn, Georgia, who first heard in sermonic form the ideas presented here, and to the church's board and staff members, all of whom have been unfailingly encouraging as I have pursued a writing ministry. I am especially grateful to Tony Evans for his writing of the foreword, and for the encouragement his life and ministry have been to me over the last three decades.

INTRODUCTION:

A PLEASANT SUNDAY AFTERNOON

As the twenty-first century dawns, the church of Jesus Christ in the Western world faces enemies by the score. One hears the word *war* often these days. We find ourselves engaged in a series of attempts to speak Christian faith into Western civilization with the outcome much in doubt. Even worse, we scramble simply to be heard at all as society attempts to marginalize Christian speech or even to exclude it from the public square. But whether we succeed or even survive in these arenas largely depends on victory in a less obvious realm, the fight for the moral life of the individual believer.

Unfortunately, Christians are losing that fight in large numbers. Our moral failures make the headlines with regularity. As I sat down to write this paragraph, a radio was trumpeting the claim of two young men that they were physically abused in a Texas orphanage operated by a local church. Unfortunately, that was just one example of many. Other indications that the moral wars are going badly:

- Recent research suggests that the divorce rate for evangelical believers now exceeds that of the population at large.[1]
- The president of a national denomination was recently sentenced to a long prison term for fraud. The painful details circulated in both Christian and secular media for many months.
- A south Florida man, a civic official and prominent member of an evangelical church, was videotaped having sex with a prostitute, after being elected on a platform of ridding his city of its vice problems.
- In recent years, several popular Christian recording artists have admitted to extramarital affairs (sometimes with each other).
- A highly regarded Christian psychiatrist, well known for urging his patients to consider biblical alternatives to traditional therapy, was discovered to have abused a number of young boys sexually over a period of several decades.
- A number of prominent pastors in recent years have been found engaging in activities ranging from theft to adultery to drug smuggling.

It has not helped that the Christian public seems infinitely willing to accept the waywardness of their Christian heroes. With few exceptions, the Christians mentioned above have continued in their ministries, experiencing scarcely a ripple in their bank accounts, performing engagements, or personal popularity. Today it is hard to imagine any behavior that could bring a sufficient degree of shame to a Christian public figure to wreck his or her ministry.

"God wants me to be happy" threatens to displace "In God we trust" as Christian America's national motto.

As a pastor, I have thought long and hard about why so many Christians today seem to have lost touch with the fundamentals of moral behavior. Some of it, undoubtedly, has come from picking up the barnacles of today's moral relativism. I have written elsewhere of the sobering degree to which believers have compromised their distinctiveness and the terrible price the church continues to pay for it.[2]

A certain percentage of the Christians in the world have always turned up their noses at biblical absolutes, of course; the New Testament bears witness to that. Never before, however, have Christians professed quite so loudly how good they feel about themselves as they sin against God. Rationalizations in support of wayward lifestyles flourish. "God wants me to be happy" threatens to displace "In God we trust" as Christian America's national motto.

Part of our moral malaise is also the disillusionment that comes when young Christians discover that while the gift of life is free, living the life can be demanding. Christian evangelists don't always tell their listeners that after their conversion their lives may become far more complicated than they ever imagined. J. I. Packer attributes such omissions to an "irresponsible kindness":

> The preacher wants to win his hearers to Christ; therefore, he glamorises the Christian life, making it sound as gay and carefree as he can, in order to allure them. But the absence of a bad motive, and the presence of a good one, does not in any way reduce the damage which his exaggerations do.[3]

As a result, people enter the Christian life with unrealistic expectations. When spiritual warfare begins, they are stunned and disillusioned. They resemble the people back in 1861 who thought that being on the fringes of a war might be fun.

That first year of the Civil War had seen little in the way of decisive action since the opening shells were fired on Fort Sumter. An impatient Northern press was issuing challenges to the administration of President Abraham Lincoln. Horace Greeley, publisher of the *New York Tribune,* loudly insisted, "On to Richmond!" Editorials in other newspapers agreed that the Civil War should and could be ended quickly. The rebels, according to prevailing opinion, would flee as soon as the Union army moved in force against the Confederate entrenchments.

In late July 1861, rumors about such an attack were rampant.

Southern troops at Manassas, Virginia, firmly in control of the railroad line leading from Washington into Virginia, received a sobering word from a Confederate spy in the capital: The Union army was about to move.

It was a poorly kept secret, in any case. Most of the citizens of Washington knew that General Irvin McDowell planned to attack the Confederate defenses on Sunday, July 21. It was so well known, in fact, that hundreds of the city's residents decided that watching the battle might be an excellent way to occupy a warm summer afternoon. So they prepared picnic baskets, dressed in their Sunday finery, and drove carriages out into the Virginia countryside to enjoy a relaxing lunch and watch the battle.

The crowds soon discovered, however, that war is not a spectator sport. The Federal troops they had come to cheer were bloodily repelled and in late afternoon began a panicky retreat toward Washington. Unfortunately, the picnickers, finally realizing their blunder, decided to head for home about the time the retreat became a rout. The hot day rapidly degenerated into a bloody, insane disaster. Civilians and soldiers snarled at each other as they competed for narrow roads and bridges while shells exploded nearby. It was a ludicrous beginning to a war that would last four terrible years.

We shudder at the naïveté of people who could possess such an unrealistic attitude about warfare. In the same way, unfortunately, many Christians fail to see, or see too late, the dreadful gravity of the spiritual battle. The casualties are all around us.

It is not that we have not been warned. The writers of Scripture often called believers to spiritual conflict. The apostle Paul, for example, likened Christian living to a daily series of individual fights. He wrote, "If by the Spirit you put to death the deeds of the body, you will live" (Romans 8:13). He spoke of the weapons of spiritual warfare (2 Corinthians 10:4) and urged his readers to put on the armor of righteousness (2 Corinthians 6:7).

Ignoring God's spiritual call to arms, however, Christians sometimes resemble picnickers more than soldiers. Perhaps that is because war is an ugly word and an even uglier idea. War leaves combatants maimed and children parentless, and few people in a combat zone escape its effects, soldiers least of all. No one likes to think about the possibilities issuing from warfare—particularly when the war is fought against enemies that are within.

Indeed, the apostle apparently believed that the bitterest of enemies lived inside himself. Those "deeds of the body" to which he referred in Romans 8:13 oppose spiritual progress in every believer. Powerful spiritual forces within us lie in ambush, waiting to punish our inattention or spiritual laxity. Christian living is not for the faint of heart.

Nor is it for the easily disillusioned. No person I've met has ever given me half as much trouble as I give myself. Spiritual progress seems to come by the millimeter. Every victory requires all the power of the Holy Spirit—the "sword" of Romans 8:13—and all my alertness and attention to the struggle. As an experienced pastor, I can say that when it comes to difficulty, nothing in public ministry can compare to the challenges of going to war with my own sinful tendencies. Simply living as a Christian calls for the best I have.

And the stakes are enormous—life and death, in fact. "If you live according to the flesh you will die; but if by the Spirit you put to death the deeds of the body, you will live" (Romans 8:13). "Living" in the apostle's thinking pertains not to eternity but to the day-to-day life of the believer. Life lived without regard to God is no life at all; it is merely a slow form of death.

Paradoxically, real living starts when we begin to challenge those acts of rebellion in ourselves that we formerly tolerated. Failure to do so means defeat; yielding to what is easy and convenient in turn produces the ugliness and stench of death. On occasion, if the Christian yields to sin often enough (or defiantly enough), such persistent moral failure may even produce premature physical death (see 1 John 5:16–17).

No Christian is pleased to find an enemy within. Everyone prefers the external variety. Believers have those, too, of course: the world and the devil. In addition to being easier to identify, external enemies do less harm to our self-esteem. It is one thing to know that satanic temptations lie in ambush down the street. It is quite another to find that those allurements find an answering chord within us. We discover that we are vulnerable, and such knowledge can prove disquieting. We would prefer to discover not only that we don't sin, but that we are not even attracted to sin. The reality is quite different.

Complicating all of this is the united voice of the culture, which encourages giving free rein to our inner impulses in the name of liberty. Christians today yield in large numbers to the siren song of personal indulgence. A former member of my church told me frankly, as I was dealing with him about his unfaithfulness to his wife, that he had missed the sexual revolution (he had married in the early 1960s) and felt cheated because of it. His current affair was an effort to make up for "lost opportunities."

French theologian François Fénelon revealed the folly in such a perspective when he observed,

> Our own passions are the worst tyrants: if you obey them but by halves, a perpetual strife and contest exists within; and if you entirely give up yourself to them, it is horrid to think to what extremities they will lead. May God preserve us from that fatal slavery which the mad presumption of man calls liberty! Liberty is to be found only in Him.[4]

Mad presumption, indeed. Yet madness is where we live. It constitutes, in fact, the environment in which all Christian growth must proceed. Our world manages to call life what the Bible describes as death, and vice versa. In the world we inhabit, spiritual poverty is viewed as true wealth and slavery to inner impulses as genuine freedom. Spiritual conflict involves being alert to these satanic redefinitions and refusing to be deceived by them.

Part of the reason that the theme of warfare appears so often in Scripture has to do with the effort, pain, and discomfort required in making spiritual progress. Battles are routinely exhausting, sometimes frantic, and always bloody events. Really doing battle with our inner inclinations involves making painful choices, and it is sometimes easier simply to go through the motions.

Another reason warfare forms such a common biblical word picture has to do with an often-overlooked characteristic of conflict. War can also produce the removal of danger and fear; indeed, that is normally its publicly stated aim. The end of a war can release people from slavery and bring gladness and prosperity just as decidedly as a conflict's onset produces death and injury. Healthy civilizations are created from war just as oppressive ones are.

This double-edged effect is one of the reasons that the Bible uses war more commonly than almost any figure of speech to summarize the way the Christian life works. Virtually every New Testament writer makes use of it. Paul included himself in the pronouns as he urged, "Let us cast off the works of darkness, and let us put on the armor of light" (Romans 13:12). Peter likewise urged his readers, "Beloved, I beg you as sojourners and pilgrims, abstain from fleshly lusts which war against the soul" (1 Peter 2:11). The apostles considered winning the inner battle to be crucial. Unfortunately, many a Christian goes AWOL from time to time.

This is a book about the spiritual fight to which God calls believers. It is, therefore, a book about conquest—the conquest of the self. My objective is to help you do battle with your worst enemy—those unseen yearnings that lie within your own breast, the vestigial impulses of what the Bible calls "the old man" (see Ephesians 4:22). The conquest of the self will never be complete this side of the Second Coming, but it is a goal toward which the Spirit of God would have us press. And along the way, if we use the weapons God provides, we will find that the struggle brings great joy with it: the joy of making progress, of seeing God at work in us and through us. From the persistent putting to death of the deeds of our bodies, we will come to know what it means to really live. The first step on the road, however, is coming to grips with the reality of the war within.

A NEW CAMPAIGN

The secret of life is to have a task. Something
that you devote your entire life to, something to
bring everything to, every minute of the day,
for your whole life. And the important thing is,
it must be something you can't possibly do.[1]
—HENRY MOORE (1831-1895), painter

Some time after the 1999 baseball season, *Sports Illustrated* featured an interview with Atlanta Braves relief pitcher John Rocker. The hard-throwing southpaw, who had made himself hated by New York Mets fans during the National League championship series, mended no fences when he issued a series of scathing remarks about those same fans, the city of New York, immigrants, and even some of his teammates.

I found people's reactions to what he said almost as amazing as the hateful remarks that provoked them. Public advice about Rocker usually contained references to psychiatrists. The recurring idea seemed to be: "What this man said could not have come from a healthy mind. He needs medical attention." Major league baseball itself finally decided that the relief pitcher should be sent for a psychiatric evaluation.

Such thinking reflects the modern Western attitude toward evil. Twenty-first century man refuses to acknowledge the notion that evil can be an innate impulse of human beings. Hurtful behavior must, according to prevailing wisdom, have an external or at least a pathological source. It must be something imposed on us by our social environment—the product of misguided parents, hateful peers, or a corrupted culture. We are much too cultured to have evil dwelling within us as an active and untamed force.

The same attitude surfaces whenever a teenager walks into a school and begins shooting his classmates. After the dead and injured are cleared out, it will only be a matter of minutes before some public official tells a television interviewer that we must discover ways to ensure that this never happens again. Suggestions for doing so generally consist of changing the physical environment of the school, installing metal detectors, teaching "conflict resolution" classes, and hiring security guards. Or people talk about influences outside the school, particularly access to guns and violent video games. The spiritual condition of the children and faculty seldom rates a mention. What could that have to do with anything?

We who are Christians often fall into a similar error, however. When it comes to our own capacities for evil, we commonly underestimate the threat that lies within our own hearts. We think of our sinful impulses as diseases like chicken pox or sinusitis: We need a cure so that we can eliminate the problem and move on. People who become Christians—especially those who believe as adults—often think that they are, as a result of their conversion, cured; or at least they suspect that it's only a matter of time until sin is simply an unpleasant memory. Then reality sets in as they experience a series of harsh encounters with temptation. Discouragement comes, at times followed by despair. We believers are astonished and disappointed to discover the strength and persistence of our evil impulses.

We shouldn't be. The New Testament was called into existence, in part, because of the horrible effects of sin in the apostolic church. Case in point: On a day in the year 56, the apostle Paul issued a warning to his perpetual projects, the bumbling Christians of Corinth. Reminding them of the spiritual disasters Israel experienced between Egypt and the Land of Promise, the apostle cautioned the Corinthians, "All these things happened to them as examples, and they were written for our admonition, upon whom the ends of the ages have come. Therefore let him who thinks he stands take heed lest he fall" (1

Corinthians 10:11–12). By the reference to falling, the apostle alerted his readers concerning the possible defection of a person who once walked with God. "Falling" happens when those who are God's children stumble away from Him to respond to the seductions of the Enemy. "Falling" in this sense is impossible for non-Christians. They have no height from which to fall. Their problem is far more deadly.

The Corinthians certainly needed the warning. More than most first-century Christians, they were prone to step in any available pothole. To forestall their tripping tendencies, Paul declared that they needed to study and heed the Old Testament accounts of the wilderness experiences of Israel. So do we. People are stumbling all around us.

After three decades of pastoral ministry, I have been witness to more examples of falling than I care to remember. I have seen church leaders fall into the clutches of immorality and greed. I have seen believers fall under the sway of neo-pagan cults and marginal Christian groups. I have seen marriages crumble under the strain of selfishness and churches dissolve from the effect of deception. If you have been a Christian for any length of time, you have observed these things too. It is beyond dispute that people outside Christian circles have been aware of them and have used them to discredit the faith we represent.

While speaking at a weekend retreat, I was asked what were the most noteworthy changes I had witnessed in my years in ministry. I was grieved to have to say that number one on my list is the enormous loss of public credibility in the American church since the early 1970s. Not only have Christians fallen, but they have fallen publicly, often, and hard. I remember a time when Christians were scorned because they chose a lifestyle that modern man considered outdated and confining. Now we are more likely to be condemned for our unfaithfulness to that lifestyle.

I am not simply referring to the well-documented catastrophes attending prominent figures in public ministry. Had we the insight of heaven, I believe we would see that the countless failures of local Christian leaders and church members have proven even more devastating in their effects. Whether great or small, we have, in the words of the ancient prophet, given the Lord's enemies occasion to blaspheme (see 2 Samuel 12:14).

LOOKING FOR SPIES

Are all those who have fallen just imposters posing as believers? The New Testament does speak of "false brethren" (Galatians 2:4); such people frequent churches all over the world and will continue to do so until Christ returns. But to place every moral failure in that category—to define "falling" Christians out of existence—seems a dishonest practice both practically and biblically. As C. S. Lewis put it, "When a man who accepts the Christian doctrine lives unworthily of it, it is much clearer to say he is a bad Christian than to say he is not a Christian."[2]

The apostles and prophets often wrote to provide counsel to those who had to deal with the aftermath of believers' failures.

Moreover, the apostle Paul calls his readers "brethren" (1 Corinthians 10:1) and "beloved" (v. 14), terms he would not have used had he been thinking of unbelievers. And if Christians cannot fall, as some suppose, what is the point of the apostolic warning to take heed? Paul even included himself in the list of people who needed to learn from the experience of Israel in the wilderness, explaining that those accounts "were written for *our* admonition" (1 Corinthians 10:11, italics added). Apparently even apostles need to learn from the mistakes of others.

Besides the biblical warnings, it is a little hard, given the present cultural climate, to see the advantage in pretending to be a Christian these days. The person who professes faith in Christ is more likely to be followed by ridicule and contempt than by any temporal advantage. An open-eyed stroll through the Scriptures shows that disappointing believers have always been around. In fact, they spurred the existence of many portions of Scripture, since the apostles and prophets often wrote to provide counsel to those who had to deal with the aftermath of believers' failures. Scripture contains examples of apparent believers who are guilty of envy, lying, murder, betrayal, incest, fornication, and idolatry—and other sins too numerous to mention.

Shaky Christians weren't exactly uncommon in Corinth. Paul warned the believers of the city not to make the mistakes of ancient Israel and "lust after evil things" (1 Corinthians 10:6). His warning presupposes that believers can do so.

And then there were those people whom Paul rebuked concerning their contempt for the Lord's Table. When Corinthian believers gathered for what was supposed to be Communion (part of a complete meal in the ancient church), some simply started eating without waiting for everyone to arrive, so others sometimes had nothing. Still worse, some members of the church drank enough wine—at the Table representing the holiest of all events on earth—to become intoxicated (see 1 Corinthians 11:21).

As you might imagine, God took a dim view of all this. As the Corinthian believers continued in such behavior, they began to experience a disproportionately large number of physical problems. Paul had to explain to them what was happening: "For this reason [your behavior at the Lord's Table] many are weak and sick among you, and many sleep [i.e., have died]" (1 Corinthians 11:30).

Divinely imposed weakness, sickness, and death—not great advertising either for a church or for its Lord—had apparently persisted in Corinth for some months. Amazingly, the Corinthians were so dense spiritually that they did not make the logical connection between the sick and dying people in the church and the congregation's behavior at the Lord's Table. Paul had to explain it to them in terms they could not miss. For some, it was too late. They passed out of their earthly existence in a state of disobedience.

At the same time, the apostle explained how such divine discipline could have been avoided: "If we would judge ourselves, we would not be judged" (1 Corinthians 11:31). Self-judgment is the divinely approved method of precluding divine judgment—or, to recall Paul's earlier statement, self-judgment is what keeps Christians from falling.

SOLDIERLY COMMONALTIES

And where did the apostle direct believers to find assistance in learning how to keep themselves upright? He took them to a place few today would consider to be a source of such help: the biblical narratives of the Exodus from Egypt and settlement of the Promised Land. He wrote: "All these things [Israel's troubles and defections] happened to them as examples, and they were written for our admonition" (1 Corinthians 10:11). Israel's flops in the Sinai wilderness, the rebellions along the way to Canaan, the failures in conquering the land—all of them were penned for you and me. God apparently thinks we can learn from negative as well as positive examples.

Although Israel's "examples" took place long ago, they touch us at many points. Think about what we who are believers, engaging in our own pilgrimage, have in common with Israel's experience during the days of the Exodus and conquest:

- We were once in bondage to a cruel taskmaster.
- We escaped from slavery and the brink of annihilation through God's miraculous provision of a deliverer.
- We are now engaged in a course of instruction in the ways of the living God.
- We are headed toward a glorious land of promise, all the while being tempted to compromise and make life easy on ourselves.
- Having seen God's mighty hand deliver us, we nonetheless find ourselves prone to complain.
- Often we hang back reluctantly although God's promises are there for the believing.
- We are engaged in a long process of putting enemies to death.
- When disciplined by God, we often panic rather than focusing on the necessary lesson.
- When challenged by unexpected obstacles, we become fearful.
- We are too easily deceived.
- We sink into apathy and forget that God placed us here for a purpose.
- We often fail to guard our minds and hearts from impurity.
- We toy with temptation and ignore sin's addictive effects.
- From time to time, we encounter giants who seem invincible.

Most profoundly of all, we discover that the capacity to ruin ourselves comes not merely from outside, but from within our own bosoms. Paul wrote to the Galatians, "Walk in the Spirit, and you shall not fulfill the lust of the flesh. For the flesh lusts against the Spirit, and the Spirit against the flesh; and these are contrary to one another, so that you do not do the things that you wish" (Galatians 5:16–17). That great comic strip theologian Pogo had it right: We have met the enemy, and he is us.

Carrying around one's own enemy poses some severe challenges, but the solution to those tyrannical inner passions begins not with denial, but with soberly coming to grips with their presence. George Whitefield, the eighteenth-century evangelist, once received a letter filled with vicious allegations about his character and the conduct of his ministry. "I thank you heartily for your letter," he responded. "As for what you and my other enemies are saying against me, I know worse things about myself than you will ever say about me. With love in Christ, George Whitefield."

Above all others, the believer ought to be able to stand the discomfort of looking into his own heart objectively, for he knows that those flaws that lie within are as doomed as the world and the devil who provoke them. Faults that manage to hang on through the years of our earthly wanderings will disappear with our old bodies. In the interim, however, we have a job to do in going to war against them.

And here we note a key point. Although many Christians are disheartened to find that they are fighting a series of inner battles, they ought not to be. Mark the impact of what Galatians 5:17 teaches: The presence of an inner conflict is a sign of genuine life. Rebirth plants the true life of God within; but because what the Bible calls "the old man" occupies the same physical home, conflict is inevitable. The Spirit and the flesh will always be at odds. We celebrate victories in individual battles from time to time, but the war will not be over until the age to come. The next time you are discouraged about your lack of spiritual progress, remember this: The difficulty of your progress gives testimony to the truthfulness of Galatians 5:17, including the reality of the Holy Spirit's presence. If Christ lives within, that battle comes from a heart that wants to do right and please God. *Not* being discouraged because you don't care is the danger sign. Indifference is the deadliest condition of all.

A MIRACULOUS TRIP TO THE FRONT

Our spiritual journey, like Israel's, began with a miracle. The wonder that shaped Israel took place along the shores of the Red Sea. God instructed the people to encamp near the water's edge, a place that was militarily indefensible: "For Pharaoh will say of the children of Israel, 'They are bewildered by the land; the wilderness has closed them in.' Then I will harden Pharaoh's heart, so that he will pursue them; and I will gain honor over Pharaoh and over all his army, that the Egyptians may know that I am the Lord" (Exodus 14:3–4). God gained a triumph at the Red Sea that was even larger than it appeared to be at the time. Israel's rescue included not only a physical victory (one that assured the continuation of Abraham's seed), but a deliverance that gave God a claim on the heart loyalty of all His people.

The events that followed the Egyptian threat are well known to us. God parted the waters of the sea, and Israel walked through safely. When the Egyptians tried to follow, they were destroyed. God did for Israel what the nation could never do for itself. He acted in grace to deliver His people from an oppressor and give them a new life.

God's law is . . . designed to show all people that they fail to conform to His standards.

The new birth is like that. It is God's work. We stand still and watch as God accomplishes a miracle in the heart by His great power. It is nothing less than the bringing of the dead to life. Even though as non-Christians we didn't feel dead, we were. God's Word tells us so. A holy God requires straight living of us, living to which we do not conform without Christ.

When my wife, Cheryl, and I moved into our first house, I began the process of trying to learn how to be a handyman—something that I have not succeeded in doing very well over the last thirty-five years. One of my first projects was to wallpaper a downstairs bedroom. Being committed to the principle of following authoritative written instructions, I proceeded through the advice of my how-to book carefully. I used a plumb bob to snap a perfectly vertical line near a corner. Since the wallpaper was a vertical stripe pattern, I knew it was important to hang the paper in a perfectly upright manner. I mounted piece after piece, edge upon edge, all the way around the room, finally returning to the corner near where I had begun. To my dismay I discovered that where the stripes met there was a rather noticeable "V" shape in the pattern. At first I thought I had misapplied a strip of paper along the way. However, a building contractor friend of mine explained that the original builder had not made the walls perfectly square. The square and the level confirmed his judgment. To the naked eye, they looked fine until I applied the wallpaper. It was only when instruments were used that the flaw became evident.

A carpenter's level cannot make a crooked wall straight, of course; it can only reveal the flaws. God's law is His level, designed to show all people that they fail to conform to His standards. It was never intended to make us straight or righteous and, indeed, it never could. It may be that you have recently become conscious that your life is not level. You may have reacted by trying even harder to observe God's standards, only to discover that you cannot keep them. If so, I have good news for you. That is one of the key reasons God gave His laws—so that we would discover that we, in and of our flawed selves, are inadequate to keep them perfectly. Happily, He did not stop there. He also sent Christ to earth to pay for the breaking of His law. He can pay for your shortcomings. He can perform a miracle and make the crooked straight; but He does so not through reform, but by the miracle of rebirth.

If you have already been reborn, your desires to do right come from the only place where it counts: the "new man" God created. Paul wrote, "Do not lie to one another, since you have put off the old man with his deeds, and have put on the new man who is [being] renewed in knowledge according to the image of Him who created him" (Colossians 3:9–10).

The "new man" also lives inside you, like the "old man," but with a difference: When the old man is gone and forgotten, the new man will still be around. He is the "new you" that God created in you, and he will never die. In other words, the long-term outcome of the conflict is not in doubt. The ultimate destiny of every believer is assured. That's why Paul used the past tense in explaining this to the Colossians: "You have put off . . . and have put on . . ." (Colossians 3:9–10). All the impulses to do right and please God that are within you come from the "new man."

Between now and the inauguration of our eternal condition, however, both the old man and the new live together inside that complex entity that we call the Christian believer. In the end, only the new man will survive; but whether he will win the inner struggle *today* has yet to be determined. That is why Paul, instead of using the past tense (as he did with the Colossians), issued orders to the Ephesians: "Put off, concerning your former conduct, the old man . . . [and] put on the new man" (Ephesians 4:22, 24). The old man cannot be reformed; he can only be put aside. The new man must, in turn, be put on. He is the clothing of the properly dressed Christian.

The Christian life begins with a miracle and continues as a series of daily battles. We already put on the new man at the moment of our conversion; but just as a soldier dons protective gear, we must re-clothe ourselves with him each moment of the day.

A NURSERY PARADOX

The new birth also shares another characteristic with Israel's experience at the Red Sea. In one respect, God's rescue of Israel was the most important event in the life of the nation. Later, and throughout Israel's history, God reminded the nation what He did for them there. At the top of the Ten Commandments sits the key reason to obey them: "I am the Lord your God, who brought you out of the land of Egypt, out of the house of bondage" (Exodus 20:2). Such reminders were necessary; Israel was terribly prone to forget His goodness.

In another way, however, the miracle at the Red Sea was the least important event in their lives. When the last Israelite stepped onto the eastern shore of the Red Sea, God had accomplished one enormous objective, but He was just beginning another. He was looking to win their hearts. That devotion could be provoked by the past, but it had to be lived every day. The Red Sea events pictured the legalities of salvation; but He wanted a great deal more. Moses summarized God's objectives as Israel was about to enter the land of Canaan:

> *Now, Israel, what does the Lord your God require of you, but to fear the Lord your God, to walk in all His ways and to love Him, to serve the Lord your God with all your heart and with all your soul, and to keep the commandments of the Lord and His statutes which I command you today for your good?* (Deuteronomy 10:12–13)

Physical birth works much the same way. Without it we wouldn't be here, but no one points back to it as an achievement. After all, somebody else did the work. Physical birth merely opens the door to a lifetime of relationships and experiences. After our birth, the growth process becomes critical; and growth, whether physical or spiritual, is invariably a painful process. Painful events and the people around us, especially our parents, help knock the rough edges off our character. God's standards of growth are more stringent, but His parental skill is correspondingly greater. Godly living, like the conquest of the Promised Land, requires a recasting of our thinking processes. We must begin to think like warriors sent to engage in a conflict—not just for one battle, but for a lifetime.

Many Christians find themselves losing their battles, however, because they approach inner warfare with unrealistic expectations. Since God brings us into His family via a miracle, we often expect that the growth process will work itself out in a similar fashion. Surely things like our addictive behaviors and tendency to complain will fall by the wayside with time, we think . . . and then reality sets in. We discover that we still have difficulty saying no to destructive habits. We find that our power to be hostile toward others hasn't left—it merely moved into the closet. We observe that we still possess a world-class ability to complain when things don't suit us. We note that our work doesn't magically do itself because we are now related to God.

Such realizations prove daunting enough to destroy some Christians. I remember a fraternity brother who came to Christ during my senior year in college. "Jerry" was one of those people who seem to be born running. His zeal for ministry and Christian fellowship was so great that he neglected his studies and found himself in big academic trouble at finals time. As zero hour approached, he implored the other Christians on campus to pray for his tests, and we did; but when the results came back, he had flunked out of school.

Although the episode might say something about the anemic nature of our prayers, it also suggested that Jerry's theology was substandard. He apparently thought that prayer was God's chosen means of bailing irresponsible Christians out of the problems they create for themselves, but his grades proved otherwise. Lots of Christians on campus, of course, exhibited the same zeal for God Jerry did; but they also applied themselves to their studies.

Alas, that was not the message that Jerry took away from the experience. He opted out of spiritual living and participation in Christian activities almost as rapidly as he had begun them. He was neither the first nor the last believer to fall because of wrong expectations.

Christians, however, have no biblical warrant for thinking that because our new birth was God's work that our growth will happen without any participation on our part. The apostle Paul attributes self-conquest to a combination of both God's work and our own: "If by the Spirit [God's part] you [our part] put to death the deeds of the body, you will live" (Romans 8:13).

I have had people argue vehemently with me about this point. "Oh, no," they say; "that isn't how it works at all. God does it all. I just let go and let God. He takes care of everything." It is hard to argue with a statement like that, for it sounds terribly pious; unfortunately, it is equally misleading. If God does it all, then He is the one responsible for it all. That means that He gets the glory when I succeed (naturally, no one objects to that), but He logically also gets the blame when I fail, and that is absurd.

I know I can count on God's resources. He has already provided me with everything I need to please Him: "His divine power has given to us all things that pertain to life and godliness" (2 Peter 1:3). When I fail, it isn't His fault—it is mine. What I can't always count on is my own willingness to use the power He provides. When I succeed, it's because He has provided me, through the Holy Spirit and the new man, with the power to do right and please Him. When I fail, it's because of my own stubbornness in refusing to engage that power—to put on the new man.

So, Christian living itself can be thought of as a holy invasion. We attempt to expel from our "land" the self-obsession that is native to our experience and replace it with a holy passion for the One who gave us life. Self-conquest involves progressively reducing the number and magnitude of those occasions when I disappoint my Lord by failing to do what pleases Him. On the positive side, it involves an ever-increasing love for Jesus Christ. Self-conquest does not mean reaching a spiritual state in which I am immune from sinning. It does mean making progress and refusing to condone or accept defeat when tests come—as they invariably will.

CHAPTER TWO

THE
ENEMY

*I do not know what the heart of a bad man is
like. But I do know what the heart of a good
man is like. And it is terrible.[1]*

—IVAN TURGENEV

The young monk with the determined look and the sheaf of papers
hurried toward the Wittenberg town square and the Castle Church.
On this October day in 1517, he had important though unpleasant
work to do, and his manner suggested that he wanted to get it over
with. Martin Luther had served on the faculty of the local university
for the past nine years. Assigned to teach the Psalms and the letters of
Paul, he had taken his responsibilities seriously; indeed, the results of
his studies had brought him to this fateful step.

Arriving at the church, he took the pages in his hand and tacked
them to the massive church door that served as the community bul-
letin board. His words called for a debate with church leaders on the
series of propositions he had just posted. History would call them *The
Ninety-Five Theses.* Though no one (not even Luther) realized it at the
time, the Protestant Reformation had begun.

At the top of Luther's list lay a proposition that was as far-reaching in its implications as it was simple in its language: "Our Lord and Master Jesus Christ, in saying 'Repent ye . . .' willed that the whole life of believers should be repentance." No Christian, the reformer implied, ever has the right to become satisfied with his moral progress. There is always work to be done. The life of faith is a life of change—a life of conflict, in fact. Those who settle for less than God intends do so at their peril. Yet many have done just that.

Sir Francis Bacon was among the most famous people in England in the early seventeenth century. A Christian and a brilliant thinker, he entered Cambridge University at age twelve and, in spite of his youth, excelled as a scholar. His subsequent accomplishments spanned the fields of law, philosophy, and science. He is often called "the father of the scientific method" and is considered by some scholars to be the real author of the plays that are usually attributed to William Shakespeare.

Bacon's gifts were more than matched by his ambition; he had a passion to rise in prominence at court and quickly did so. In 1603, he was knighted and thereafter became in turn solicitor-general, then attorney-general, then Lord Keeper of the Great Seal. His public career reached its apex when he was named Lord Chancellor of England, a position that had been occupied by Thomas More, Thomas Becket, and other luminaries.

Along the road to greatness, however, he failed to guard his moral life. His secret sins and gigantic ambition began to rule him—and then ruined him. He was impeached by Parliament for taking bribes. As a result, he was disbarred and banished from the city of London. He left public life a broken and disgraced man.

Bacon was neither the first nor the last Christian to fail in the public eye. He made the mistake, as many have done, of thinking that his worst enemies in life were external. The real opponent of the Christian, unfortunately, never tires, never sleeps, and lives within him. Like Francis Bacon and like ancient Israel on the way to the Promised Land, many of us discover this the hard way.

THE "ITES" HAVE IT

When Israel came to the borders of Canaan, God identified the nation's enemies as "the Hittites and the Girgashites and the Amorites and the Canaanites and the Perizzites and the Hivites and the Jebusites, seven nations greater and mightier than you" (Deuteronomy 7:1). These nations were essentially the same people who had lived in the land when Abraham first arrived there. God had promised Abraham that the land of Canaan would in time belong to his descendants. Even after God delivered Israel from Egypt, however, it still took more than seventy years before Abraham's offspring held title to most of the Promised Land. Though the "—ites" they faced were formidable, their inner weaknesses proved an even greater hazard.

Before Israel even crossed the Jordan, King Balak of the Moabites hired a prophet named Balaam to curse the Israelites as they passed through Moabite territory. Numbers 22–24 explains how Balaam found himself unable to carry out his commission, and Israel remained uncursed. What an external enemy could not accomplish unaided, however, an internal one could. God's ire was aroused by Israel's own behavior:

> *Now Israel remained in Acacia Grove, and the people began to commit harlotry with the women of Moab. They invited the people to the sacrifices of their gods, and the people ate and bowed down to their gods. So Israel was joined to Baal of Peor, and the anger of the Lord was aroused against Israel.* (Numbers 25:1–3)

An enemy greater than the Moabites had brought Israel to ruin.

THE OLD MAN

The enemy of the Christian cannot be seen, but no thinking person would deny his reality. Called "the old man," or "the flesh" by the apostle Paul, he lives within us during our natural lives. His existence goes back to the fateful choice made by our original parents to declare their autonomy from God. Since that time, man's independent streak has been part of his nature—and we have been paying a high price for it.

Only when one becomes a Christian, however, does he fully feel the force of the old man's presence. The apostle Paul described it in a telling passage: "I am carnal, sold under sin. For what I am doing, I do not understand. For what I will to do, that I do not practice; but what I hate, that I do. . . . But now, it is no longer I who do it, but sin that dwells in me" (Romans 7:14–15, 17). That's an *apostle* talking.

The sin that I so despise dwells in me. Please note: *sin, not sins.* Sins merely form the outward expression of an inner power. As much as I would love to rid myself of my rebellious nature, I can't. I carry it everywhere I go.

Dr. Philip Blaiberg was one of the world's first heart transplant patients. After his operation his surgeon, Dr. Christiaan Barnard, asked, "Would you like to see your old heart?"

Blaiberg said yes, and Barnard took him to the room in the hospital where the heart was being stored. The surgeon took down a glass container from the shelf and handed it to Blaiberg. As the first man ever to hold his own heart in his hands, Blaiberg pondered the amazing sight for a while and finally said, "So this is my old heart, that caused me so much trouble." He handed it back to Dr. Barnard, then turned away and left the room.[2]

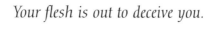

Your flesh is out to deceive you.

Our old inner self, unfortunately, cannot be dismissed so readily. The old man is inescapable; he is also relentless in drawing me away from God. Not only that, he is bad and getting worse. He "grows corrupt" (Ephesians 4:22) daily. Nothing good issues from him. I can't improve his behavior; I can only replace it with the behavior of the "new man": "Put off, concerning your former conduct, the old man which grows corrupt according to the deceitful lusts . . . and . . . put on the new man" (Ephesians 4:22–24). That is the way we progress in Christian living. We get dressed spiritually every day by putting off the old man and putting on the new.

Since I can neither rid myself of the old man nor reform him, the only sensible approach to doing battle against him is to use and strengthen the inner assets I have that oppose him. The asset that Paul mentions in his analysis of the old man and his effects is the mind: "For I delight in the law of God according to the inward man. But I see another law in my members, warring against the law of my mind" (Romans 7:22–23). The mind is critical in the conquest of the self because the basic approach of the flesh is deception. That is the stock-in-trade of the Enemy, and if you are going to believe God and get in the fight, know for sure that your flesh is out to deceive you. The basic approach of the flesh, in fact, is deception: "Each one is tempted when he is drawn away by his own desires and enticed. Then, when desire has conceived, it gives birth to sin; and sin, when it is full-grown, brings forth death" (James 1:14–15). Our impulses can be lethal—for ourselves and for others.

The Skillfulness of His Deceptions

Do you ever wonder how it is that people who have a long history of walking with the Lord are captured in a transgression? At least part of the answer comes from God's analysis of the human condition: "The heart is deceitful above all things, and desperately wicked; who can know it?" (Jeremiah 17:9–10).

The "heart" in this passage is simply another way of referring to the flesh. You will never have an opponent as skillful as your own heart. We have a terrible enemy living inside us, and we carry him everywhere we go. That is why, upon conversion, God counters this powerful presence within us by two of His own. He creates a new person within us, the "new man," (Ephesians 4:24), and He gives us His Spirit. These changes do not mean that victory is inevitable, merely that it is possible; and they mean that if we don't win it is not because God failed to provide us with the weapons. We always have to be alert for the inner ambush.

After everything crumbled around him, Francis Bacon wrote a prayer in which he confessed his sins and acknowledged that he had wrecked his life by ignoring the condition of his inner person. He wrote: "I may truly say, my soul hath been a stranger in the course of my pilgrimage."

We cannot afford to have our souls be strangers. God intends that we study ourselves and learn our weaknesses. We ought to be experts concerning our vulnerabilities. If we know that we have a weakness in a certain area, we cannot allow ourselves to come within reach of temptations in that realm. We must have respect for the skillfulness of the flesh's deceptions.

However, even if you become well aware of your weaknesses, you will never be immune to surprises. From time to time you will be blindsided. How do I know this? Because Jeremiah's passage tells me that no one can fully understand himself: "The heart is deceitful . . . who can understand it?" The question is purely rhetorical.

The Vehicles of His Deceptions

The old man uses our longings to do us harm. The inner urges that are part of our flesh reach out to get a grip on us. That is why Paul wrote, "Put off . . . the old man which grows corrupt according to the deceitful [desires]" (Ephesians 4:22). The cravings of our inner person he characterizes as "deceitful."

Our desires deceive us. They tell us that if we could only indulge ourselves and gratify a particular desire, we would be happy people. So we indulge ourselves, and guess what? We're not happy at all. In fact, often we are less happy than we were before we indulged, for we now are not only disappointed, but we are also guilty. The flesh has again lied to us. Wrong desires always hold out a promise that they never deliver. Nothing sinful is ever as good as it promises to be.

The Effect of His Deceptions

A primary effect of the flesh's deceptions is to harden us and make us less likely to trust and obey God in our next battle. Evil habits as well as righteous ones are strengthened by practice. That is why the author of Hebrews wrote, "Exhort one another daily, while it is called 'Today,' lest any of you be hardened through the deceitfulness of sin" (Hebrews 3:13). Sin deceives us by setting us into patterns—by "hardening" us.

The British poet Samuel Taylor Coleridge serves as a case in point. Col, as he was known, was born in England about the time of the American Revolution. The son of a minister, he was a brilliant young man, having something of a photographic memory; and, like Francis Bacon, Col quickly distinguished himself as a scholar. His best-known work, "The Rime of the Ancient Mariner," is a dark study in sin and remorse. Coleridge knew about both.

As a young man, he suffered several health problems and his physician prescribed laudanum to ease them. Laudanum is an opium preparation, and Coleridge became addicted to it. All his life he struggled against it, especially after he was converted at age forty or so; but he was never able to overcome his enslavement. Late in life he wrote of his struggles:

> I used to think the text in James that "he who offended in one point, offends in all" was very harsh; but I now feel the awful, the tremendous truth of it. In the one crime of opium, what crime have I not made myself guilty of!—Ingratitude to my Maker! And to my benefactors injustice! And unnatural cruelty to my poor children!—self-contempt for my repeated promise-breach, nay, too often, actual falsehood.[3]

Coleridge's "crime of opium" destroyed his marriage and ruined the life of his daughter, who also became addicted. Sin deceived him into building his life around his indulgence—a life that could only be characterized as a miserable one. Before he died, he wrote a short poem to serve as his epitaph and express his misery. It reads,

> *Beneath this sod*
> *A Poet lies; or that which once was he.*
> *O lift one thought in prayer for S.T.C.*
> *That he, who many a year with toil of breath,*
> *Found Death in Life, may here find Life in Death.*

What a sad waste! Hardened by the deceptions of his desires, he went to his grave a captive. Sin, fully matured, brought forth death (James 1:15). Hardening comes when sin's deceptions set us into destructive patterns—what the Bible calls wrong or false ways. Freedom usually cannot be gained without help in such cases. As the writer of the epistle to the Hebrews knew (see Hebrews 10:23–25), part of the answer is mutual encouragement as the battle progresses; but prevention is better still, as David prayed: "Search me, O God, and know my heart; try me, and know my anxieties; and see if there is any wicked way in me, and lead me in the way everlasting" (Psalm 139:23–24). There is a strong feeling in that prayer that try as he might, David could stumble in his fight—as we know he did.

LEARNING TO WALK

The key to avoiding stumbling in the inner war is learning to walk spiritually. Just as we learn to walk by using both legs, Paul explained to the Ephesian Christians that spiritual self-conquest requires a combination of two processes: "Put off . . . the old man . . . put on the new man" (Ephesians 4:22, 24). When a person becomes a Christian believer, he or she has to learn to walk all over again: "You should no longer walk as the rest of the Gentiles walk" (v. 17).

Walking, more than anything else, is our declaration of independence as human beings. It is when we begin to walk that we begin to become our own persons; yet learning to walk is a risky business. We learn by tilting our bodies forward and starting to fall, then catching ourselves by taking a step—by informed experimentation, in other words. We see others do it, we take some chances, and before long we have learned to walk.

That's how Christian living works too.

Step one is negative. We begin to walk when we turn away from behavior we know is displeasing to God. Paul calls it *putting off*, saying no to sinful actions and attitudes. The world at large—and a significant percentage of the church, sad to say—thinks that Christian morality is satisfied by this first negative step. Christians are people who don't do certain things. If you asked a hundred non-Christians today what is the distinctiveness of Christians—what sets them apart from the world—many would answer with a negative description: Christians don't drink; Christians don't smoke; Christians don't gamble; Christians don't engage in extramarital sex.

The world (at least some of it) consequently thinks of us as a group of people who specialize in self-control. They might in some cases grudgingly admire us because they know how hard it is to exercise self-control themselves. But they don't see anything attractive in us. All they see is the avoidance of pleasures, and they want no part of it. But "putting off" by itself is the equivalent of trying to walk with one leg. It is difficult, and what you do can't really be called walking in any genuine sense.

Step two, however, is positive. Paul doesn't just insist on putting off; he also talks about putting on. If putting off is the removal of sinful behavior, putting on is the replacement of sinful behavior by virtuous behavior. In God's instructions about how Christians are to walk we find negatives and positives side by side. In Ephesians 4, Paul describes four specific strides Christians can make, and in every case the negatives and the positives appear together.

Handling Conflict

Part of walking is learning how to handle conflict. In Ephesians 4:25, the apostle places two steps side by side:

Negative: "Put away lying."
Positive: "Speak truth with [your] neighbor."

These two steps are intended to break down barriers to communication caused by conflict. As the apostle knew, Christians lie to each other regularly. When someone hurts me, do I tell him the truth about it? No, I keep it bottled up inside, or—even worse—tell a close friend how I have been wronged. He, in turn, passes the news along (so that others might pray more intelligently, of course). Now several people are estranged.

The apostle says that when we become Christians that has to stop. When a significant offense occurs—one serious enough that we think about it through the day—we have to go to the offending party and tell him the truth; and even in our pain we must express the truth in a righteous way: "Be angry, and do not sin" (Ephesians 4:26). Most important of all, we have to refuse to let our anger settle into a hardened habit and become a grudge. Paul continues, "Do not let the sun go down on your wrath" (v. 26). In other words, settle each dispute on the day it occurs. If we don't do this, we let the devil embed his hooks in us. We have violated Paul's warning in the same context: "[Don't] give place to the devil" (v. 27). When you become resentful against anyone, you are giving the Enemy leverage to exploit you and disturb the peace of God's church.

Taking Responsibility

Learning to walk also means taking responsibility for our own economic well-being and for being a help to others. In Ephesians 4:28, Paul brings together negative and positive commands:

Negative: "Let him who stole steal no longer . . ."
Positive: "but rather let him labor."

Economic responsibility means more than just paying our own bills. The Christian works so that "he may have something to give him who has need" (Ephesians 4:28). The Christian believer who says, "I'm going to earn enough money to pay my bills and that's all I'm going to worry about" is dishonoring the Lord and has not yet learned to walk as he should. We are supposed to have as our goal the saving of money so that we can invest it in others, to provide for worthwhile ministries and people who have needs.

I was embarrassed in 1999 by the behavior of some parts of the Christian church in America as we exhibited a significant ignorance of these fundamental precepts. We began badly by predicting world-wide chaos as the year 2000 began (one prominent Christian teacher flatly predicted a billion deaths). Christians were advised to accumulate cash and to hoard food. Some people even suggested that we retreat into the mountains with our accumulated supplies and money, taking guns and ammunition so that we could be ready to beat off the assaults that would come when people began to starve. It was disappointing to see Christians leading the way in such every-man-for-himself attitudes. Where would you and I be if Jesus Christ had taken the attitude that self-preservation was the goal of living? A better approach would have been to show some simple prudence against the uncertainties along with the goal of being able to share with others who found themselves in need—a lifestyle that is always proper for believers.

Producing Encouragement

In Ephesians 4:29, we learn that aspect of walking that touches our speech:

Negative: "Let no corrupt word proceed out of your mouth . . ."
Positive: "but what is good for necessary edification, that it may impart grace to the hearers."

Hurtful words have to be eliminated. Even more important, we need to substitute positive, encouraging ones. We are to speak in ways that supply "necessary edification"—a lovely redundancy. Edification, the building up of people, is always necessary, and for two reasons. First, it is a beautiful way that Christians can show themselves obviously distinct from the world. We ought to lead the way in being encouraging, positive people in the eyes of those around us. The world has a way of tearing people down. We ought to build them up. We don't have to praise everything that we see in other people, but if we look with Christ's eyes we can nearly always find something that is praiseworthy and encouraging. When He wrote the letters to the seven churches of Asia (Revelation 2–3), He almost always began by providing encouragement before issuing necessary rebukes.

---

*We learn to walk only as we replace
the harmful with the edifying.*

Another reason that edification is necessary is that we are all vulnerable people. We know our faults better than anybody. We feel them intensely. There should be one group of people in the world who will encourage us—not that believers conspire to tell lies, but that we see in each other what God has placed there.

EXHIBITING TENDERNESS

Part of walking as a Christian is learning how to exhibit Christ-like attitudes. Again, notice the pairings in Ephesians 4:31–32:

Negative (v. 31): "Let all bitterness, wrath, anger, clamor, and evil speaking be put away from you, with all malice."
Positive (v. 32): "Be kind to one another, tenderhearted, forgiving one another, even as God in Christ forgave you."

In the negative step, the first five expressions describe what we see: bitterness, wrath, anger, clamor, evil speaking. The last expression is why they are there: malice. Hostile attitudes are the source of everything else. Hostility and malice are always out of place for Christians. On the other hand, kindness, tenderness, and a forgiving spirit, while rare in the world, ought to be common among believers.

C. S. Lewis summarized the importance of the paired steps of Christian morality this way:

> If you asked twenty good men today what they thought the highest of the virtues, nineteen of them would reply, Unselfishness. But if you asked almost any of the great Christians of old he would have replied, Love. You see what has happened? A negative term has been substituted for a positive, and this is of more than philological importance. The negative ideal of Unselfishness carries with it the suggestion not primarily of securing good things for others, but of going without them ourselves, as if our abstinence and not their happiness was the important point.[4]

God's purposes in the world are not merely to suppress or inhibit sin. His purposes are to raise up a group of people who exhibit and extol His virtues and cleave to Him totally. Simply avoiding sinful behavior may conform to truth, but it provides no beauty. People are not drawn to those with strong self-control; they are drawn to people who exhibit kindness, tenderness, and a forgiving spirit. We learn to walk only as we replace the harmful with the edifying. If our lives are filled with hurtful words, those have to be replaced by healing ones. We have to go out of our way to strengthen and encourage people. It is only when we do that that we are walking as the body of Christ, increasingly exhibiting the victories of our inner warfare.

Martin Luther had it right. Christian living provides an unlimited scope for spiritual change. Like Moses, Joshua, and Israel approaching Jericho, the whole land is before us. The conflict is real; life and death are hanging in the balance. God wants us to move forward even with the uncertainties that lie ahead, and we dare not settle for less than He offers.

CHAPTER THREE

BATTLE CRY

*Christianity is a statement which,
if false, is of no importance, and if true,
of infinite importance. The one thing
it cannot be is moderately important.*[1]

—C. S. Lewis

During the rest of this book we will be looking closely at the Old Testament narratives of Israel's movement from Egypt to Canaan—what Paul described as an account filled with examples of a wrong approach to spiritual living. You may be wondering: "Why would God use something as bloody and violent as the conquest of the Promised Land as a picture of Christian living?" The two may not even seem compatible to you. In fact, to some people, devoting any thought to the Israelite conquest of Canaan is repulsive. They have been told that the whole event is a regrettable and disgraceful episode: A vast, murderous, warlike nation (Israel) invades the land west of the Jordan and slaughters multitudes of people who are minding their own business. To the modern ear, it smacks of racism and a sort of divinely approved hatred.

Some people are bothered so much by the accounts, in fact, that they begin to look for ways to divorce God from the whole process.

The Hebrew invaders, they reason, coveted the land of Canaan and the riches of the Canaanites so greatly that they invented theological justification for the Conquest after the fact. They put words into God's mouth that gave divine authority for what they did. That way, they could feel better about themselves and excuse their bloodthirsty and merciless behavior. Before going more deeply into the subject of self-conquest, it will be worth our while to take a closer look at the nature of the Conquest while seeking answers to these assertions.[2]

A CONTROVERSIAL CONQUEST

The part of the argument that says Israel, after the fact, invented God's instructions to invade the land may be well-meaning, but it creates a bigger problem than it attempts to solve. At first blush, God's instructions do seem contrary to what we know of Him from the rest of Scripture: "When the Lord your God brings you into the land which you go to possess, and has cast out many nations before you . . . and when the Lord your God delivers them over to you, you shall conquer them and utterly destroy them. You shall make no covenant with them nor show mercy to them" (Deuteronomy 7:1–2).

The problem, however, is this: "What we know of God from the rest of Scripture" is equally threatened by the argument. If Moses or the Israelites put words into God's mouth to justify the invasion of Canaan, who is to say that Peter and John did not put words into Jesus' mouth describing God's love and mercy? There is as much documentary evidence for one as for the other—to be precise, no evidence at all. Ultimately, the whole approach is just a little too convenient. It opens the door for the deletion of any teaching that makes us uncomfortable; and once you establish the precedent, there is no logical stopping point.

However, even for the person who acknowledges that the biblical text reflects God's instructions, there remains a level of discomfort. How are we to reconcile, "Blessed are the merciful, for they shall obtain mercy" (Matthew 5:7) with "You shall make no covenant with them nor show mercy to them" (Deuteronomy 7:2)? How are the love and patience of God compatible with the instruction, "Of the cities of these peoples which the Lord your God gives you as an inheritance, you shall let nothing that breathes remain alive, but you shall utterly destroy them . . . just as the Lord your God has commanded you" (Deuteronomy 20:16–17)? It is impossible to exclude women and even children from the latter command. Are we to conclude that God found pleasure in the death of children when Israel invaded Canaan?

WHAT HAPPENED IN THE CONQUEST

It helps define the issues more clearly to compare God's instructions about the Conquest with other "severe" actions on His part. The flood of Noah, for example, marked a time when God acted in judgment against sinners. I find that far fewer people are disturbed by the events of the Flood than by the conquest of Canaan, though the number of deaths in the Flood was incomparably greater. Why? Probably because at the Flood God acted without human intermediaries in exacting His judgment. No human being was involved in drowning people when the waters of the Flood covered the earth. The same observation can be made concerning His judgments against Sodom and Gomorrah. No human produced the cataclysm that buried those two cities of the plain and destroyed their inhabitants.

At the Conquest, however, humans who were themselves sinners acted as God's agents in His judgment against sin. Indeed, here lies the first answer to criticisms about the Conquest: The Canaanites deserved judgment, and God used Israel to accomplish that judgment. Somehow, people are disturbed less by God's exacting judgment against the Canaanites (or Amorites, a term often used synonymously) than by His using Israel to do so. Nevertheless, it is a well-established biblical principle that when God judges sinners, He frequently uses other sinners in the process.

But did the Canaanites/Amorites deserve judgment, even annihilation, for their crimes? Did they deserve being singled out for destruction? Yes. God says as much, and the historical record supports His indictment.

Canaanite civilization (and I use the term loosely) proved to be one of the most degraded cultures in human history. The Canaanites practiced, among other things, child sacrifice. Children were offered to pagan deities not only during "sacred" ceremonies but also when

Canaanite cities were threatened (usually by foreign armies). For example, Egyptian bas-reliefs from the Late Kingdom depict the capture of towns in Palestine and show besieged people tossing their children from the city walls to placate the gods.[3] They even offered up children when laying the foundation stones of houses or cities, a practice that may have been imitated by at least one Israelite (see 1 Kings 16:34). The Canaanites engaged in child sacrifice in spite of the fact that surrounding cultures generally deplored it.

Incest was also common in Canaanite society. The evidence is found in Scripture itself. Leviticus 18 contains a long list of prohibited sexual unions between close relations. The motivation for these specifications reads, "Then the Lord spoke to Moses, saying, 'Speak to the children of Israel, and say to them: "I am the Lord your God . . . according to the doings of the land of Canaan, where I am bringing you, you shall not do. . . . None of you shall approach anyone who is near of kin to him, to uncover his nakedness: I am the Lord" (Leviticus 18:1–3, 6). Even the Canaanite deities as portrayed in their religious literature were often incestuous and undoubtedly inspired these practices (or was it the other way around?). Except for the Egyptians (and then only among the nobility), incest was frowned upon in surrounding cultures.

Bestiality, outlawed by most ancient near Eastern law codes, was practiced by the inhabitants of Canaan and reflected in the abhorrent practices of the very deities they worshiped. The same can be said for homosexuality, which was rampant and even part of religious observance (though, unlike other Canaanite practices, homosexuality was countenanced by surrounding nations).

Cult prostitution (both male and female) formed a basic part of Canaanite society. Though surrounding societies often criticized the practice, the Canaanites considered it fundamental to their culture and were always ready, as the invading Israelites discovered, to share such "religious" joys with newcomers.

One writer summarizes Canaanite civilization at the time of the Conquest by saying, "By 1400 B.C. the Canaanite civilization and religion had become one of the weakest, most decadent, and most immoral cultures of the civilized world."[4] Even worse, the Canaanites refused to apologize for their depravity and instead sought to bring others within the circle of their debased religion.

Were the Israelites so morally advanced as a nation that they were entitled to put this culture to the edge of the sword? Absolutely not. God told Israel,

> *Do not think in your heart* . . . "Because of my righteousness *the Lord has brought me in to possess this land"; but it is because of the wickedness of these nations that the Lord is driving them out from before you. It is not* because of your righteousness *or the uprightness of your heart that you go in to possess their land, but because of the wickedness of these nations that the Lord your God drives them out from before you.* . . . *Therefore understand that the Lord your God is* not *giving you this good land to possess* because of your righteousness, *for you are a stiff-necked people.* (Deuteronomy 9:4–6, emphasis added)

Three times in three verses, the Lord emphasized that they should avoid the wrong conclusion. God was using an imperfect instrument to effect His judgment, just as He later used the Babylonians to judge the people of Judah and drive them out of the land (see Habakkuk 1:1–13) when they adopted Canaanite religious practices.

The people of Israel were to act as God's instrument of judgment simply because He commanded them to do so. As we will see, they found the assignment so irksome that they failed to carry it out. Far from being enthusiastic and bloodthirsty about their responsibilities, the Israelites dragged their feet and avoided obeying God's commands—to their everlasting regret.

The Canaanite Body Count

Had Israel carried out God's instructions, however, far less blood would have been shed than one might think. A careful reading of the divine instructions for the Conquest yields a number of surprises. For starters, better than a dozen different verbs are used in those instructions, and some of them do not appear to be compatible with each other. For example, Deuteronomy 20:16–17 contains the severe imperative, "Of the cities of these peoples which the Lord your God gives you as an inheritance, you shall let nothing that breathes remain alive, but you shall *utterly destroy* them . . . as the Lord your God has commanded you" (italics added).

On the other hand, Numbers 33:51–52 gives rather different instructions: "When you have crossed the Jordan into the land of Canaan, then you shall *drive out* all the inhabitants of the land from before you" (Numbers 33:51–52, italics added). There is, of course, a world of difference between "driving out" people and "utterly destroying" them. A concordance study reveals that the command to "drive out" the Canaanites occurs more frequently than any of Israel's other instructions, accounting for about three out of every four imperatives. How are we to understand the relationship between "driving out" and "destroying"?

The easiest reconciliation is to see *expulsion* as applying to the people in general and *destruction* to the leaders of the society (living primarily in the walled cities). Several considerations support this view. For example, God repeatedly reminded Israel that the inhabitants of the land of Canaan outnumbered them. In Deuteronomy 7:1, He refers to "seven nations greater and mightier than you." Later, He repeats, "You are to cross over the Jordan today, and go in to dispossess nations greater and mightier than yourself" (Deuteronomy 9:1). Since Israel included (counting women and children) between 1.5 and 2 million people, we are probably accurate in considering the sum total of the nations occupying the land as a figure somewhat larger than that.

However, the biblical record suggests that the number of deaths came nowhere near this figure. When Joshua described the victories of Israel during the Conquest (Joshua 12), he included in his final list of conquests the names of thirty-one cities. The ruins of many of these have been found. By measuring the circumference of the walls, a rough estimate may be made of the number of the cities' inhabitants. According to most scholars, a typical Canaanite walled city measured only five to twenty acres[5] and held between one and three thousand inhabitants. Doing the math, thirty-one times three thousand yields a maximum body count slightly over ninety thousand. That is a long way from (at least) two million. How do we account for the difference?

The answer lies in recognizing that God's intent was for Canaanite society to be destroyed at the same time the Canaanite people—the vast bulk of them, living in the open countryside—were driven out of the land. The people who lived in the walled cities were the kings, merchants, and priests of a corrupt society. They had the most to lose, and they would be the most reluctant to leave. Thinking themselves secure inside their fortress walls, they would have held out to the last.

On the other hand, farmers living in the country would have known their vulnerability to armed invasion. Rather than see their families threatened, many of them would simply have pulled up stakes and moved away. This likelihood would have been increased with each passing year and with each successive Israelite victory. When Jericho fell, for example, the road to the interior of the country lay open. Many of the people in the hill country of Judah must have decided that they would at least move beyond the reach of the imminent battles.

Remember that Israel had been out of Egypt for forty years before setting foot in the Promised Land. It would not have taken long for the word to get out that an army of 635,000 was headed toward Canaan. Knowing that they intended to settle in the land after driving out its people probably produced many a conference between local mayors.

*The Canaanites, having had years
to anticipate the Conquest, had a choice.*

Rahab, a harlot from Jericho, summarized the understanding of the Canaanites when she told the Israelite spies, "I know that the Lord has given you the land, that the terror of you has fallen on us, and that all the inhabitants of the land are fainthearted because of you" (Joshua 2:9). She recognized that Israel's assets included more than simply battle experience:

> *For we have heard how the Lord dried up the water of the Red Sea for you when you came out of Egypt, and what you did to the two kings of the Amorites . . . whom you utterly destroyed. And as soon as we heard these things, our hearts melted; neither did there remain any more courage in anyone because of you.* (vv. 10–11)

Her words reflect not only an awareness of the dangers involved from the Israelite invasion but the fact that others in Canaanite society shared her apprehension.

As a result of this knowledge, the people of Canaan had been preparing for the invasion for years. For many of them, I am sure, the choice was easy: better to be refugees outside the land than wait around for annihilation. Even people in the cities would have been tempted to get out, and I am sure many did. At the very least, they probably evacuated many of their women and children—particularly after Israel utterly destroyed the first walled city, Jericho. It is probably safe to say that far fewer than 90,000 people died during the Conquest, and that those who did perish were the people who had the deepest attachment to the depraved Canaanite cult. Ultimately it was the leaders who posed the biggest threat, concerning whom Moses said, "He will deliver their kings into your hand, and you will destroy their name from under heaven; no one shall be able to stand against you until you have destroyed them" (Deuteronomy 7:24).

> *The pockets of Canaanite society that remained in the land proved able to infect all of Israel.*

What I am suggesting here is that the Canaanites, having had years to anticipate the Conquest, had a choice. They could leave, or they could stay where they were and risk destruction in the cities—and it is uniformly the cities that are described in the accounts of the Conquest as having suffered destruction. God's instructions, then, were aimed primarily at expelling the Canaanites and destroying the leaders of Canaanite culture and thus the culture itself.

The Purpose of Expulsion

From Israel's perspective, the idea behind the Conquest, after all, was twofold: (1) to fulfill the promises made to the patriarchs, and

(2) to give Israel a home without having them sucked into the moral depravities of Canaan. Thus, the *culture* had to be destroyed, though the *people* could be expelled. As long as the cult existed, Israel was in peril: "You shall make no covenant with them nor show mercy to them. Nor shall you make marriages with them. You shall not give your daughter to their son, nor take their daughter for your son. For they will turn your sons away from following Me, to serve other gods" (Deuteronomy 7:2–4). God hammers on this theme all through the account of the Conquest. The people of Israel will be corrupted by their own mercy if they extend it to the Canaanites.

Which is, of course, precisely what happened.

The pockets of Canaanite society that remained in the land proved able to infect all of Israel. The kings and people of the northern tribes drank deeply of Canaanite religion and were, seven centuries later, themselves deported. Eventually, even the kings of Judah, the descendants of David, sacrificed their own children in the fire to pagan deities, and God traced the practice back to the Canaanites:

Ahaz the son of Jotham, king of Judah . . . reigned sixteen years in Jerusalem; and he did not do what was right in the sight of the Lord his God, as his father David had done. But . . . he made his son pass through the fire, according to the abominations of the nations whom the Lord had cast out from before the children of Israel. (2 Kings 16:1–3)

When the idolatry and depravity of Judah reached the depths in the sixth century before Christ, God brought the Babylonian army against His people. Jerusalem fell after a long and terrible siege, and Judah marched into seventy years of Babylonian captivity.

To prevent this defection God issued a stern warning that helps clarify the nature of the Conquest of Canaan. He said, "Do not defile yourselves with any of these [sexually immoral practices]; for by all these the nations are defiled, which I am casting out before you. For the land is defiled; therefore I visit the punishment of its iniquity upon it, and *the land vomits out* its inhabitants" (Leviticus 18:24–25, italics added). Apparently, the "punishment" God had in mind consisted of expulsion.

In fact, the same punishment later came upon Judah, in accordance with God's warning:

You shall therefore keep My statutes and My judgments, and shall not commit any of these abominations . . . lest the land vomit you out also when you defile it, as it vomited out the nations that were before you. For whoever commits any of these abominations, the persons who commit them shall be cut off from among their people. (Leviticus 18:26, 28–29, italics added)

In other words, God held Israel to the same standard that He used in judging the Canaanites, and that judgment would be visited on Israel if the Israelites violated it. The judgment against Israel would consist of the land "vomiting out" its inhabitants—in a word, expulsion. The people of Judah were not annihilated; they were deported. Israel might have deported the Canaanites, too, but at the time of the invasion of Canaan Israel had no homeland to which to deport them.

A Dangerous Assumption

To be sure, humanity finds the Conquest of the Promised Land irksome. In one way, so does God. Scripture affirms that judgment is God's "unusual act" (Isaiah 28:21) since He engages in it so rarely. We enjoy His kindness, designed to give us scope for repentance (Romans 2:4), and after a time we come to believe that we deserve to be treated in grace and kindness indefinitely. But the fact that God does not often deal with men as they deserve does not mean that He must never do so. Judgment may be His unusual work, but it is still His work.

The Lord Jesus, justly famous for His gentleness and the universality of His love, affirmed this understanding at a tense moment during His earthly ministry. Apparently, a group of Galileans had gone to Jerusalem to worship. While they were in the temple grounds, some of Pilate's guards had come upon them and (for reasons unknown) had slaughtered them as they were in the process of offering sacrifice. The Galileans had thus become martyrs in the eyes of the public. When the report came to Jesus, He commented in a way that took His hearers by surprise: "Do you suppose that these Galileans were worse sinners than all other Galileans, because they suffered such things? I tell you, no; but unless you repent you will all likewise perish" (Luke 13:2–3).

The questioners had fallen into the illusion that is universally held by modern man: God has no right to bring people to violent ends just because they are sinners. They must be advanced and accomplished sinners—Hitlers or Stalins or Jeffrey Dahmers—to experience His judgment.

That conclusion, however, is not warranted by logic; it is only suggested by experience, and our experience reflects a knowledge of God's persistent grace and gentleness, not of His prerogatives. When, on rare occasions, sinners perish because of His judgment, observers often indict God for the wrongness of His actions. However, according to the Lord Jesus, a better response would be repentance.

No Other Standard

A still more basic issue looms behind this entire discussion: God is the source of all legitimate ethical norms. Who He is and what He teaches constitutes the only true basis for evaluating any kind of human behavior. He cannot be held accountable by some external standard; He *is* the standard. As Abraham asked, "Shall not the Judge of all the earth do right?" (Genesis 18:25).

The occasion for that question was a revealing one. Abraham was conversing with the Lord as He walked toward Sodom to verify the city's susceptibility to judgment. God had taken an intimate interest in the town, insisting on a personal inspection of their waywardness before allowing destruction to come. Had even ten righteous people been found in Sodom, He agreed, the city would not be destroyed.

Only Lot was found righteous in Sodom, however. The place fell far short of the ten needed to preserve it. In spite of the rather shaky spirituality of Lot and his family, God spared their lives.

Sodom proved an example of how God proceeds on those exceptional occasions when He acts in judgment against significant numbers of people. His judgments occur only after long periods of warning and witness to the truth. Lot may not have been a great evangelist, but at least the people of Sodom recognized him as an evangelist (see Genesis 19:7–9). Before judgments fall, individuals like Lot and Rahab—and the Canaanites—find that God has provided an avenue of escape. In wrath, God remembers mercy.

Canaan had experienced a long history of exposure to the truth, beginning with Abraham centuries before and Melchizedek even earlier (see Genesis 14:18–20). Avenues of escape lay in every direction as Israel sluggishly approached over a whole generation. Even after the invasion began, it proceeded slowly, allowing people still more time to escape. This was in part by divine design. Moses explained to Israel, "The Lord your God will drive out those nations before you little by little; you will be unable to destroy them at once, lest the beasts of the field become too numerous for you" (Deuteronomy 7:22). The snail's pace of the invasion suited the Lord and benefited both Israel and the Canaanites.

In a revealing passage, God showed the measure of His patience with the inhabitants of Canaan. More than five centuries earlier, the Lord had solemnized a covenant with Abram in a dramatic way. Putting His servant into a kind of trance, God issued a prophecy about the destiny of Abram's offspring:

> *Then He said to Abram: "Know certainly that your descendants will be strangers in a land that is not theirs, and will serve them, and they will afflict them four hundred years. And also the nation whom they serve I will judge; afterward they shall come out with great possessions. Now as for you, you shall go to your fathers in peace; you shall be buried at a good old age. But in the fourth generation they shall return here."* (Genesis 15:13–16)

If at that instant the groggy Abram wondered why it would take four hundred years before his descendants returned from Egypt, the Lord quickly explained with a telling statement: *"for the iniquity of the Amorites is not yet complete"* (v. 16b, italics added). Israel could not return until *the time that the moral degradation of Canaan had proven so terrible that the earth itself could not tolerate it.*

Abram may have thought—especially in view of their sometimes harsh treatment of him—that the Canaanites were guilty enough already; but the mercy of God is far larger than that of man (see 2 Samuel 24:14). By the time Israel arrived on the eastern bank of the Jordan, the wickedness being practiced inside the borders of the Promised Land had reached a horrible apex.

For Our Instruction

Is all this of interest merely to scholars and ethicists? Hardly. The biblical account of the Conquest paints a terrible picture of *incomplete dedication to a critically important task.* The way Israel carried out its assigned responsibilities fell far short of what God had ordered. The people of Israel disobeyed God's instructions by permitting pockets of fanatical pagans to remain among them. The people of God placed themselves in jeopardy by their own natural reluctance, once the population of a region had largely fled, to finish the distasteful business, lay siege to the cities, and execute the remaining leaders. In the accounts of the Conquest, God did not condemn Israel for their bloodlust in the Conquest. He rebuked them for thinking so little of their spiritual lives that they would allow a small but flinty core of Canaanites—people who would prove to be among the greatest religious advocates in world history—to remain in each part of the land.

We should not extend mercy to our moral weaknesses, but instead drive them out pitilessly.

What applies to us, of course, is the attitude reflected in the divine design for the Conquest. The severity that God commanded Israel to exercise in Canaan provides a picture of how a Christian believer is to approach his moral life. No compromise can ever be permitted when it comes to living a life of righteousness. Our eye should not allow any trace of rebellion to remain within.

The Conquest was a bloody and distasteful time, to be sure. So is going to war against our old man. Progress in Christian growth is a slow, painful, and often trying business. Disappointments lie at every turn. The enemy is heavily entrenched and fortified, and our resolve often seems weak.

We should not extend mercy to our moral weaknesses, but instead drive them out pitilessly. Toward other people, we must be tender and forgiving; but against the enemy within us we must be unsparing. The militant believer's battle cry can be summarized in two words: *No mercy.*

CHAPTER FOUR

COMMAND
AUTHORITY

Tonight Shanghai is burning
And I am dying, too
But there's no death more certain
Than death inside of you
Some men die of shrapnel
Some go down in flames
Most men die inch by inch
While playing little games

—UNKNOWN[1]

During the 1930s, Communist dictator Josef Stalin ordered that all Bibles and all Christian believers be eliminated from the Soviet Union. His lackeys sent the premier's edict in every direction across that vast land. When the order reached Stavropol, thousands of Bibles were confiscated and their owners were dragged away to prison camps, where most died. The confiscated Bibles, however, stayed in warehouses for half a century.

After the fall of the Iron Curtain and the relaxation of attitudes about people of faith, a Christian missionary organization sent a team to Stavropol to carry out several ministry projects. In order to accomplish their work, they asked for a load of Bibles from Moscow, a shipment that was delayed in arriving. While they were waiting, someone explained to one of the team members that a whole warehouse full of

Bibles remained in the city from Stalinist days. But no one was sure if the government would be willing to release them.

The team assembled and prayed about the matter. The shipment from Moscow still hadn't arrived, so they decided to inquire about the confiscated Bibles. They were indeed where they had been for fifty years, officials said, and yes, if the missionaries could use them they were welcome to take them and distribute them throughout the city.

So, the next day the missionaries rented a truck and drove to the warehouse. To assist in loading the truck they hired several locals, one of whom was a surly, hostile young man who made it clear he had come only for the wages. During the course of loading the truck, this young skeptic disappeared. The missionaries looked for him for a long time, finally discovering him sitting in a corner of the warehouse weeping.

A determination to recognize and heed God's Word forms the bedrock of all progress in the spiritual battle.

It seems that in the course of loading the Bibles, the young man had decided to take one for himself. When he opened it, he was stunned to find on the inside of the front cover the signature of his own grandmother, a woman who had been among those persecuted believers of Stavropol in the 1930s. Her testimony had, through the tender providence of a loving God, reached across the years to pierce his heart in a way that nothing else could have.[2] The packaging of God's message had given it an added authenticity.

One of the prerequisites of self-conquest is a conviction that mastering the old man is possible because God has commanded it. A determination to recognize and heed God's Word forms the bedrock of all progress in the spiritual battle. When God wanted to encourage Israel, He often cut short all discussion by saying, "Have I not commanded you? Be strong and of good courage; do not be afraid, nor be dismayed, for the Lord your God is with you wherever you go" (Joshua 1:9). Unfortunately, many Christians treat God's imperatives merely as a signal to open negotiations. When God brought Israel out of Egypt, however, He took steps to encourage Israel's recognition of His authority over their moral choices. The way He did it shook them to their foundations. As with the young man in Stavropol, the method He chose to deliver His truth gave it instant credibility.

I was asked once whether it was plausible that someone might have invented God long ago out of a passionate desire to have Him exist. In other words, cannot we account for Christianity and all theistic religions on the simple basis of wish fulfillment? No doubt man can invent his own gods and has done so repeatedly. But the inventions of pagans bear little resemblance to the God of Scripture. No one would choose to invent the God of the Bible even if he could, because the moment he did so he would be forfeiting his autonomy, the nearest and dearest possession of humanity. Anyone who was at Mount Sinai could have testified that the God who revealed Himself there was a Person who settled all questions of authority simply by unveiling His character.

GOD PRESENTS HIMSELF

Almost immediately after rescuing Israel from Egypt, God brought Israel to the mountain to hear His Word. Israel stayed at Sinai longer than at any other single location on the way to Canaan. For about nine months—from Exodus 19 to Numbers 9—the nation was gathered to attend the Word of God as it was given to them directly.

Most people find the idea of God speaking directly highly desirable. A lot of us think (at least secretly) that hearing an audible voice from heaven would impress us more than simply reading the words of Scripture. God, on the other hand, apparently doesn't think that direct revelation is best for most people, because only a small percentage of believers have ever heard His voice in that way. Sinai, however, was an exception.

Israel had gathered at the base of Mount Sinai to hear God speak. He first issued what we call the Ten Commandments, with special effects that would make Cecil B. DeMille hang his head in shame. As Israel listened and watched with an increasing awe, God's words were accompanied by thunder and lightning; the mountain was smoking, the earth was quaking, and the nation heard the distant (and increasing) sound of a trumpet—a sort of divinely provided fanfare for what

God had to say. God took as His first task, if you will, letting His people know of His power and authority. When He said, "Have I not commanded you?" He wanted them to know the power of that "I."

The spectacular phenomena of Sinai served as God's way of getting Israel's attention. They could scarcely deny that they were hearing His words (see Deuteronomy 18:16); and while the content may have been welcome, the speaking itself scared the daylights out of them. "They trembled, and stood afar off" (Exodus 20:18). They felt deeply their creaturely limitations when God revealed His Word directly. So they asked Moses to serve as an intermediary: "You speak with us, and we will hear; but let not God speak with us, lest we die" (v. 19). At Sinai we find a nation privileged to hear God's voice . . . and they sincerely hoped it would never happen again.

A few ill-informed people have criticized them for this. They shouldn't have been such wimps, their critics say. They deferred to Moses when they should have been getting their truth directly from God. If only they had been sufficiently spiritual, they would given Moses the day off.

The way we receive God's truth is critical.

If all we had to go on was the account in Exodus 20, that might—emphasize *might*—be a valid criticism. However, we don't have to guess about God's opinion of their petition. Forty years later, Moses recalled the episode for the second generation on the eve of their invasion of the Promised Land. He reminded the nation of its earlier request for an intermediary, recalling what God had said in response:

I have heard the voice of the words of this people which they have spoken to you. They are right in all that they have spoken. Oh, that they had such a heart in them that they would fear Me and always keep all My commandments, that it might be well with them and with their children forever! (Deuteronomy 5:28–29, emphasis added)

The people's discomfort with the way God delivered His message did them credit. They recognized their creatureliness and His holiness—which was precisely what He wanted them to know.

God spoke directly to them—exactly what we think we would want Him to do—but the people did not find it comfortable . . . nor would we. If God spoke to us today as He spoke at Sinai, all of us would be shielding our faces on our hands and knees; and God would be pleased that we feared Him enough to do that.

Yet Mount Sinai is a scene that is repeated in every Christian life. God refuses to allow vagueness in matters of authority to go unchallenged. The way we receive God's truth is critical, for it reveals the opinion we have of Him. Paul recalled how the Thessalonian believers received it when he wrote, "We also thank God without ceasing, because when you received the word of God which you heard from us, you welcomed it not as the word of men, but as it is in truth, the word of God, which also effectively works in you who believe" (1 Thessalonians 2:13). When we welcome the Word of God as coming from Him, it works in us effectively. It changes us from the inside out. When we treat His truth as just more information, however, little happens.

It is the Word of God that brings us face-to-face with the scope of the battle and the greatness of our Commander. If we are paying attention, we come to see that self-conquest poses a larger challenge than we are first inclined to think. Likewise, the more clearly we see God, the more we appreciate the divine assets He provides for the struggle. As C. S. Lewis observed:

> When a man is getting better, he understands more and more clearly the evil that is still left in him. When a man is getting worse, he understands his own badness less and less. A moderately bad man knows he is not very good; a thoroughly bad man thinks he is all right. . . . Good people know about both good and evil: bad people do not know about either.[3]

How we receive the truth goes a long way toward determining how fit we will be for the spiritual struggle. But some of us still think God should put His Word to us in a form that commends it and makes it impossible to ignore. We wait for God to impress us before we will take Him seriously. Yet God doesn't ordinarily reveal His Word in the manner He did at Sinai. Only one generation saw the marvels in the wilderness. Only one generation observed the drama of the smoking mountain. Most of the people who lived even in Old Testament times heard (or read) the Word of God as it had been passed down from their spiritual ancestors—which is, of course, how we receive it.

In the normal scheme of things God gives mankind His Word in a form that calls attention to its content, but not its power. The power surfaces in due time; but at the beginning, it is the content that we notice. God provides it through a mediator so that we can handle its content without being frightened by its delivery. That is a mark of His grace. He loves us, and He packages His Word in a form that we can tolerate.

The people requested that He do so at Sinai too: "You go near and hear all that the Lord our God may say, and tell us all that the Lord our God says to you, and we will hear and do it" (Deuteronomy 5:27). The people were wise enough to know that they needed a mediator. In Moses, they had a good one.

We need a mediator, too; and we have the best. The Lord Jesus is the one Mediator between God and man. As a true human being, He knows all that we are—all our weaknesses, all our shortcomings, and all our pains. So He can represent us perfectly before the Father. He intercedes for us as we engage in our warfare against the flesh. If He didn't, we would make no progress at all. Because He serves as our Mediator, we are privileged to see God at work in our hearts as we persist in the spiritual battle. The changes He makes may seem unspectacular to others, but to us they testify to the reality of His interest in us. They persuade us of His command authority.

The people at Sinai knew of God's interest in them; they knew equally that His interest in them did not give them the right to be flippant about Him. As we go about the painful business of putting the flesh to death, we do well to walk that same narrow but safe pathway. Jesus Christ knows our weaknesses and intercedes for us—but He is also the One whose face is like the midday sun (see Revelation 1:16). The way we think of Him and approach Him in worship is critical.

THE GOD WE WORSHIP

As part of Israel's education in God's command authority, God explained how they were and weren't to approach Him. Lest they approach Him inappropriately, He cautioned them, "You shall not make anything to be with Me—gods of silver or gods of gold you shall not make for yourselves" (Exodus 20:23). Humanly crafted images of God find no place in legitimate worship. Man cannot sit down and invent a valid approach to God; he will always twist it into an unrecognizable shape. Nor can he jettison the divine initiatives of the Word in favor of humanly invented connections with heaven; still, we try.

Many counselors and pastors have had the experience of having counselees or parishioners try to escape personal responsibility by leaning on claims of direct revelation. Some of those who complain find themselves in complicated and difficult marriages and suggest that "the Lord is leading" them to leave their mates (without biblical justification). Others, having been wronged in business dealings, explain that Paul's prohibitions against suing other Christians (1 Corinthians 6:1–8) don't apply to them, for "the Lord has shown" them otherwise.

These sad episodes betray the fact that Christians often prefer to short cut the difficult business of getting to know God on His terms. We are like the people who buy diplomas from Websites; we want the degree without doing the work. God ordinarily will not let us get away with taking shortcuts to a knowledge of Him.

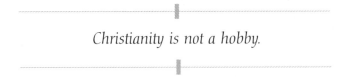

Christianity is not a hobby.

When professing Christians bypass God's revelation of Himself in His Word and invent their own approach to Him, they violate the basic precepts of Sinai: "If you make Me an altar of stone, you shall not build it of hewn stone; for if you use your tool on it, you have profaned it" (Exodus 20:25). To profane something is to make it ordinary or common. God says, "You may think you are able to craft a suitable approach to Me, but you can't. You have to do it the way I tell you, or you'll be building a worship system like all the pagan systems in the world. It will be common; it will be profane—just like everyone else's paganism." God expects us to be the joyful recipients, not the originator. Jesus paid it all, not 99 percent of it.

God speaks from heaven to tell us that He has already done for us everything that is needed for us to be right with Him. We not only don't need to do any trimming of stones to make Him an altar, if we do it ourselves we will ruin everything. If we trimmed the stones on the altar, we would spend time bringing people to the altar and saying, "Look at those beautiful stones I trimmed!" We merely need to accept the work that God has done for us in Christ and use the tools He gives us to do the interior reconstruction that He expects. God has already made the way to Himself and designed it so that we will see how terrific He is. Knowing who we are and who He is helps us to see that we cannot regard the God of heaven as just another option when it comes to deciding how we live.

In the post-Watergate era, at a time when heroes have all been knocked off their pedestals, believers in the Western world often struggle with placing anyone in a position of absolute authority. We have been burned too often. A major leap of progress in self-conquest comes when we finally decide that Christianity is not a hobby. We cannot be satisfied with possessing a faith; we must have a faith that possesses us. Our Commander is a jealous God, and properly so. Having second place in our lives will not suffice.

A motivational speaker once gave a lecture at his local high school. The speaker talked for a while about priorities and then said, "OK, time for a quiz." He placed a one gallon wide mouthed jar on the table in front of him. Then he produced about a dozen fist-sized rocks and carefully placed them, one at a time, into the jar. When no more rocks would fit inside, he asked his observers, "Is this jar full?" Everyone in the class said yes.

The speaker responded, "Really?"

Reaching beneath the table, he pulled out a bucket of gravel, which he carefully poured into the jar, shaking the jar periodically and causing pieces of gravel to fall into the spaces between the larger rocks. After this exercise, he again asked the group, "Is the jar full?"

"Probably not," one of them answered. They were catching on.

"Good!" he replied.

Again reaching under the table, he produced a bucket of sand. As he poured the contents into the jar, it filled the spaces between the rocks and the gravel. Once more he asked the question, "Is this jar full?"

"No!" the group shouted.

Again the speaker said, "Good!"

Grabbing a pitcher of water, he poured it in until the jar was filled to the brim. Then he looked up at the class, paused for dramatic effect, and asked, "What is the point of this demonstration?"

One student raised his hand and said, "The point is, no matter how full your schedule is, if you try really hard, you can always fit some more things into it!"

"No," the speaker replied, "that's not the point. The truth this illustration teaches us is this: If you don't put the big rocks in first, you'll never get them in at all."[4]

God told Israel in no uncertain terms—speaking from heaven itself—that He was the one and only option when it came to authority in their lives. He required that they give Him priority in their lives. He wanted them to pay attention when He spoke. He wanted them to approach Him in humble recognition of who He was and who they were. And if they were really smart, they would take their allegiance a step further. They would burn their spiritual bridges behind them and commit themselves to a relationship of loving service.

THE GOD WE SERVE

This book was born in Africa. Its first chapter came together as my wife, Cheryl, and I spent two weeks in Kenya where I spoke to a conference of Bible translators. They had gathered to worship, receive encouragement from the Word (my part), and plan. All of them were working with tribal groups living in what was (when they began work) the nation known as Zaire. Today it is called the Democratic Republic of the Congo.

Whatever it is called, the nation has been bleeding for years. A civil war continues there as I write, keeping the translators in nearby countries, hoping that soon they can return and be reunited with the people they love and get on with the work in their villages.

During their spiritual life conference, each translator told the challenges he or she currently faced, and then another led the group in prayer for those needs. In most cases, the prayer requests were significant. Several had lost all their earthly possessions as they had to flee for their lives from marauding armies. One had been attacked by a deadly viper, had lost much of a thumb, and had suffered the lingering effects for many months. Paul and Kathy Schmidt, longtime friends of ours and missionaries from our church, had a mortar shell explode under the crankcase of their four-wheel drive vehicle, brought to their village at great expense. They had also lost their home and all their household goods. Many of the translators had escaped invading armies by the narrowest of margins. In one case, soldiers were entering the village while the plane sent to rescue the missionaries circled overhead, waiting for a signal that it was safe to land. For many of the missionaries, it was not their first emergency evacuation.

Not the slightest trace of self-pity was mingled with any of these accounts. If anything, there was a measure of sorrow that they could not bear their hardships with better grace. The one common thread that ran through every testimony was an intense longing to see their friends in the village again and to be able to continue with their translation efforts.

It was a humbling experience for me. I wondered how I could help such people who had suffered so much more for their faith than I ever have. I was reminded of the wistful remark by an English bishop who mused that when the apostle Paul arrived in a community, riots often ensued; when *he* showed up, people served tea.

None of those translators, however, would consider himself or herself heroic. They were doing exactly what they wanted to do. What we consider to be heroic efforts in ministry ultimately issue from an inner commitment to put one's future entirely in the hands of the God of heaven. It is the only logical thing to do, when you think about it. The apostle Paul called it our "reasonable service" (Romans 12:1).

THE GOD TO WHOM WE SUBMIT

One eighteenth-century Moravian missionary left his comfortable home and traveled to the West Indies to take Jesus Christ to those slaves who worked the sugar plantations. After years in the attempt, he had seen almost no results. The slaves endured hard labor all day in the fields. By the time they returned home in the evenings, they were exhausted and longed only for food and sleep. Adding to the physical barriers, the slaves often endured merciless treatment and had, as a result, developed an understandable bitterness toward Europeans.

The missionary, however, proved he was a man hard to discourage. He prayed often that God would allow him to see a breakthrough in his attempts to witness about Christ to those unfortunate people. As he was pondering the challenges of evangelism to the slaves, a thought occurred to him. Suppose he sold himself into slavery . . . yes, that might just do it. It would remove, at least, two of the biggest barriers. The slaves would no longer be able to identify him with their captors, and he could talk to them while they worked instead of trying to reach them when they were exhausted.

He decided to do it. Slowly, over time, his fellow slaves came to trust him and believe his message. What the message could not do unaided, embodied love accomplished. Hundreds became Christian believers because of his enslavement to Christ.

As Israel was gathered below Mount Sinai, Moses issued a statute providing a picture of a similar devotion—the devotion God is looking for from believers (see Exodus 21:2–6) in their daily battles with themselves. The legislation allowed a Hebrew to become a perpetual slave—voluntarily. The idea may have struck them as odd (at least), but after the first generation of Israelites died in the wilderness, Moses repeated the instructions so that the new generation wouldn't miss them. He wrote: "If your brother, a Hebrew man, or a Hebrew woman, is sold to you and serves you six years, then in the seventh year you shall let him go free from you" (Deuteronomy 15:12).

Such servitude was ordinarily caused by poverty (see Deuteronomy 15:11). When a Hebrew couldn't pay his bills, he could sell himself into slavery to help offset his financial shortcomings. Everybody understood that these arrangements were temporary. In the seventh year, the slave-of-necessity went away not only with his debts paid, but with a considerable degree of wealth: "When you send him away free from you, you shall not let him go away empty-handed; you shall supply him liberally from your flock, from your threshing floor, and from your winepress. From what the Lord has blessed you with, you shall give to him" (Deuteronomy 15:13–14). So much might be expected.

Then comes the surprising provision: "And if it happens that he says to you, 'I will not go away from you,' because he loves you and your house, since he prospers with you, then you shall take an awl and thrust it through his ear to the door, and he shall be your servant forever" (Deuteronomy 15:16–17).

This Mosaic provision suggests what the rest of Scripture teaches explicitly: Man is incomplete until he finds a Master he can delight in loving and serving. Absolute freedom, the passion of our age, is an impossibility for a creature: "A creature revolting against a creator is revolting against the source of his own powers—including even the power to revolt. . . . It is like the scent of a flower trying to destroy the flower."[5]

Ever since Eden, man has been in a mad pursuit of those pleasures without which he deems himself incomplete, and finding that they do not exist in the places where they are reputed to be. Oscar Wilde, who did it all, admitted as much: "The gods have given me almost everything. But I let myself be lured into long spells of senseless and sensual ease . . . I ceased to be lord over myself. I was no longer the captain of my soul, and did not know it. I allowed pleasure to dominate me. I ended in horrible disgrace."[6]

Paul, choosing a different path, gloried in calling himself Christ's slave: "Paul, a bondservant of Jesus Christ" (Romans 1:1). It takes some of us years to see the wisdom in Paul's proud and paradoxical boast that slavery to Christ is the only way to find real freedom. The conditions for being able to say that are found in God's provision for voluntary slavery in Israel.

A Submission Based on Knowledge

Only a person who had the ability to evaluate his happiness as a temporary slave could become one permanently. The person described in Deuteronomy certainly did. He had served his master for six years.

At the end of the period, he knew precisely what it meant to serve in that household. The Christian slave must likewise know what he is getting into, and experience will, in time, supply that knowledge.

We might ask, "Why did God say that a voluntary slave should be distinguished by having a pierced ear?" Any number of marks might have been made on a person, but God specified the ear. Why was that?

Part of the answer no doubt has to do with the ear's visibility. A person who had committed himself to perpetual slavery made a public testimony of that fact when he submitted to having a permanent mark made on his ear. However, some of the purpose likely has to do with the role of the ear in obedience. A slave's hearing is how he both gets to know the master and discovers the master's will. The centerpiece of the Law of Moses is Deuteronomy 6:4, which begins, "Hear, O Israel . . ."

Hearing is where devotion begins. If you would voluntarily submit to the yoke of Jesus Christ, the first order of business is hearing what He has to say. Submission must be based on knowledge and experience.

We should listen to what other people have to say about being yoked to the Lord Jesus and learn from it too. We can read in the New Testament the words of people who were slaves of Christ. We probably know people in our own experience who can be properly thought of as slaves of Christ. We ought to profit from their example. The best teacher, however, is seeing the kindness of God in our own experience. In the legislation in Deuteronomy, the voluntary slave knows what he's getting into, because he has been the master's slave for six years. He knows how he has been treated, and that makes him want to make the association permanent.

If you will think about it, you can see how this little part of God's law addresses something significant. For most people, conversion and voluntary enslavement are events that do not happen simultaneously. Occasionally they do, but only occasionally. The conversion of the apostle Paul, who never looked back, is hardly typical. Most of us have to have a period of experience with the Lord before we are willing to think about making our slavery a permanent arrangement.

Unfortunately, for many a Christian the commitment to be the slave of Christ is never made; and until a believer determines whom he serves there will be dimensions to Christian living and of self-conquest that will be closed off to him. For most of us, we have all the experience we need to make that choice. We know deep down that there is no value in a selective or intermittent kind of submission to Christ. And if we desire to be consistently successful in our conquest of self, we may find it impossible until we cross this bridge.

A Submission Built on Love

The bridge is built on pillars of love for Christ. The Mosaic provision specifies a love-based submission: "If it happens that he says to you, 'I will not go away from you,' because he loves you and your house . . ." (Deuteronomy 15:16). That of course, is the only way to make voluntary submission work in the end. We will never submit to the gentle yoke of Christ, or if we do we will not stay submitted, unless we love Him supremely.

*He condescends to woo us, rebels all,
with a seeking, passionate pursuit
that causes angels to hold their breath.*

Interestingly enough, several old hymns that have fallen into oblivion used this text in Deuteronomy. One of them contains the following poetic testimony of Frances Ridley Havergal:

*I love, I love my Master;
I will not go out free;
For He is my Redeemer
He paid the price for me.*

*I would not leave His service
It is so sweet and blest;
And in the weariest moments
He gives the truest rest.*

He chose me for His service
And gave me power to choose
That blessed perfect freedom
Which I shall never lose.

Rejoicing and adoring
Henceforth my song shall be
I love, I love my Master
I will not go out free.

The heart attitude reflected in that hymn was what God was looking for, in the end, from Israel. Moses said as much as he gave the nation God's final exhortation before they entered the Promised Land: "You shall fear the Lord your God; you shall serve Him, and to Him you shall hold fast, and take oaths in His name. He is your praise, and He is your God, who has done for you these great and awesome things which your eyes have seen" (Deuteronomy 10:20–21). As He did with Israel, God takes the initiative in blessing us. He condescends to woo us, rebels all, with a seeking, passionate pursuit that causes angels to hold their breath.

Mel Trotter was a slave to drink, and he knew it. He had come by it honestly, born into the home of a man who was likewise an alcoholic. His life had spiraled downward from the day that his addiction became the central feature of his consciousness. The low point in his life came on an evening in 1897 after his daughter's death. Trotter, desperate for alcohol, reached into her casket at the funeral home and removed the shoes from his little girl's feet. He then left, walked down the street, and pawned the shoes for money to buy another drink.

As he stood that day in a downtown Chicago saloon thinking about the state of his life, he reached a decision: The world would be better off without him. He stumbled out of the saloon and headed toward the waterfront, determined to end his life in the icy waters of Lake Michigan. On the way, a doorman at the Pacific Garden Mission invited him in for the evening service. He staggered to a seat and heard a mission worker present God's plan of salvation. Responding to the message in faith, he was joyously converted.

Born into the faith with a burden for people like himself, he began to tell his testimony and became a regular speaker at PGM services. His marriage and his life slowly began to heal. The change in Mel was so dramatic that people in Chicago often referred to him as "the happiest man in the world." He devoted the rest of his life to meeting the needs of the indigent, establishing sixty-seven rescue missions from Boston to San Francisco.

The driving force in Mel's life was the knowledge that the One who had done "great and awesome things" in his life had a right to expect all his devotion. As he could testify, no one who has offered his ear to God's awl has ever been disappointed. It is the only reasonable thing to do.

CHAPTER FIVE

ENCAMPMENT

My conscience hath a thousand several tongues,
And every tongue brings in a several tale,
And every tale condemns me for a villain.[1]
—SHAKESPEARE

Marcel Sternberger had been living in the New York area for years, and he knew how important it was to be methodical. A transplant from Hungary, he took the 9:09 train of the Long Island Railroad every working day of his life to the Woodside station, where he transferred to the subway to travel into Manhattan. However, on the morning of January 10, 1948, he decided quite impulsively—and out of character—to visit a sick friend in Brooklyn instead. Spending the morning with his friend, he then took a city-bound subway toward his office on Fifth Avenue. Finding the subway car crowded, he first thought he would have to stand all the way into town, but a man sitting nearby suddenly rose to leave, and Marcel took the vacated seat.

He noticed as the car started to move that the man in the next seat was reading a Hungarian newspaper. He decided to strike up a conversation with the stranger (again, something he rarely did) by addressing the man in Hungarian. Marcel's seatmate proved quite talkative and especially glad to be conversing in his native tongue.

His name was Bela Paskin and he had been in the United States only a short time. As the subway car moved toward downtown, he told the sad story of how he had come to be in the country. Bela had been conscripted into a labor battalion by the German army during World War II and had been sent to the Ukraine.

After the war ended, he walked many miles to return to his home town of Debrecen in eastern Hungary. Arriving at the apartment where his family had lived, he found that they were gone, and no one could tell him their whereabouts. Likewise, visiting the apartment that he and his wife had occupied prior to the war, he found unfamiliar faces and blank looks; no one knew anything about his wife.

As he walked out of the building in a rapidly increasing gloom, his spirits were lifted when he encountered a boy who had been a neighbor. He accompanied the lad home and heard from the youngster's parents some terrible news: Bela's family was dead, victims of the Nazi death camp at Auschwitz. He also learned that his wife had been taken to Auschwitz, but there had been no news of her. Heartsick and nearly without hope, he made his way to Paris and obtained permission to immigrate to the States, where he had arrived only three months before.

As he listened to Bela Paskin's sad narrative, Marcel Sternberger recalled hearing a strikingly similar story only a few weeks before. It had come from a young woman he had met at the home of some friends. She, too, had lost her family to the Nazi death camps and had been forced to work in a German munitions factory for a time; more significantly, her home town had also been Debrecen, Hungary. Marcel probed his memory, but couldn't recall her name. Then he remembered that he had written it down. Flipping through his address book, he found the entry. As calmly as he could, he asked Bela, "Was your wife's name Marya?"

Bela's jaw dropped: "How did you know?"

The two men left the train, Marcel leading Bela to a nearby phone booth. Marcel dialed the number in his address book. Once Marya had answered the phone, Marcel handed the instrument to his new friend and watched as Bela, with tears in his eyes, spoke to the wife that he had feared was lost forever. As the two conversed, Bela was so emotionally overwrought that finally Marcel took the phone and asked Marya to stay put while he sent her husband to her. He recalls:

> At first I thought I had better accompany Paskin, lest the man should faint from excitement, but I decided that this was a moment in which no strangers should intrude. Putting Paskin into a taxicab, I directed the driver to take him to Marya's address, paid the fare, and said good-bye.
>
> Bela Paskin's reunion with his wife was a moment so poignant, so electric with suddenly released emotion, that afterward neither he nor Marya could recall much about it. . . .
>
> "Even now it is difficult to believe that it happened. We have both suffered so much; I have almost lost the capability to not be afraid. Each time my husband goes from the house, I say to myself, 'Will anything happen to take him from me again?'"
>
> Her husband is confident that no horrible misfortune will ever again befall them. "Providence has brought us together," he says simply. "It was meant to be."[2]

We are thrilled by such a dramatic evidence of God's compassionate and skillful hand in bringing a separated couple together. Yet Israel knew God by still more tangible evidences than the providential connection that reunited Bela and Marya Paskin. When the nation traveled between Egypt and Canaan, God chose to lead it in a wonderful, direct, and spectacular way. When He wanted the camp to pull up stakes and move, the visible symbol of God's presence (either the cloud by day or the pillar of fire by night) would move away from the camp in the direction He wanted them to go. For example, when the people of Israel left Mount Sinai after their nine-month sojourn there, "they departed from the mountain of the Lord on a journey of three days; and the ark of the covenant of the Lord went before them for the three days' journey, to search out a resting place for them. And the cloud of the Lord was above them by day when they went out from the camp" (Numbers 10:33–34).

Many of us think we would enjoy having each detail of our lives decided for us as Israel did in the wilderness. It appears to us such a simple and straightforward way to live. For Israel, however, it seemed to bring a great many drawbacks. The most bothersome aspect of God's leading was His annoying habit of taking Israel to places that were uncomfortable. The two common characteristics of these episodes were uncomfortable surroundings and complaining.

Complaining is a practice that God evaluates rather differently than we do: "When the people complained, it displeased the Lord; for the Lord heard it, and His anger was aroused. So the fire of the Lord burned among them, and consumed some in the outskirts of the camp" (Numbers 11:1). We may consider complaining a harmless error, a simple expression of rights guaranteed by the First Amendment. In the Sinai, however, God considered it a capital crime. Nor was this the only occasion when people died on account of their whining. Paul reminded the Corinthians later, "[Let us not] complain, as some of them also complained, and were destroyed by the destroyer" (1 Corinthians 10:10). In the last passage, griping is laid alongside idolatry, sexual immorality, and tempting the Lord as a crime worthy of death. God's providential provisions are special gifts, and ought not to be held, as Israel held them, in contempt.

Engaging in conquest of the self, like moving toward the Promised Land, is a process that often provides opportunities for complaint. We complain about the slow state of our growth, about our health, our bank account, and our job without ever seeing the similarity between our situation and Israel's. It seems obvious to us that we would worship God more enthusiastically if these difficulties could simply be resolved. We see them as issues that interfere with our single-minded devotion to God rather than providing the environment in which that devotion is to be expressed. The Israelites thought that real life would begin when they had conquered the land. From God's point of view, however, their life was beginning on the trip, as He sought to gain their hearts and used discomfort as a teaching tool.

While reading the stories of Exodus and Numbers, it is easy to think, *If I had been there, I wouldn't have complained.* The best test of that question, however, is whether or not I am complaining now. The Spirit of God is continually leading us too, but His concerns are not with a visible homeland but with spiritual change. If we are able to follow His leading in the spiritual battle without complaining, then we are making progress in self-conquest.

What Israel complained about more than anything else was manna, the unusual food that lay on the ground each morning of Israel's trip to Canaan. The fact that it kept the travelers alive didn't stop them from groaning about it. They wanted more variety in their diet. After two or three months, their food seemed so repetitive. I mean, how many ways can you fix manna? They had it fried, roasted, boiled, fricasseed, grilled, sautéed, and poached and then started the cycle again. For forty years in the Sinai wilderness, no husband ever popped his head into the tent and asked, "What's for dinner, dear?"

HEAVENLY FOOD

Reading the accounts from this safe distance has a way of romanticizing them too. Manna seems much more delectable when the taste buds have had a chance to recover. Fourteen centuries after the travels in the wilderness, the people of Israel asked Jesus Christ to provide manna for them as a proof of His Messiahship: "What sign will You perform then, that we may see it and believe You? What work will You do? Our fathers ate the manna in the desert; as it is written, 'He gave them bread from heaven to eat'" (John 6:30–31). Memory has a way of playing tricks on people. What their fathers found appalling, they considered appealing.

The Lord Jesus saw through this superficial demand—which, after all, was merely a modernized form of complaining about His ministry—and called their bluff:

Moses did not give you the bread from heaven, but My Father gives you the true bread from heaven. For the bread of God is He who comes down from heaven and gives life to the world. . . . I am the bread of life. He who comes to Me shall never hunger, and he who believes in Me shall never thirst. (John 6:32–33, 35)

Jesus is all the spiritual food that you and I will ever require. When He leads us into battle with ourselves, He supplies all the spiritual nutrients that we need to sustain us. The manna of Israel provided a wonderful illustration of that principle. Six weeks after leaving Egypt, the food the people had brought with them began to run out. They complained to Moses and Aaron in a typically overstated way: "Oh, that we had died by the hand of the Lord in the land of Egypt, when we sat by the pots of meat and when we ate bread to the full! For you have brought us out into this wilderness to kill this whole assembly with hunger" (Exodus 16:3). God responded by His provision of manna, a lovely picture of the sufficiency of Christ for daily trials.

Measured

Among the most noticeable features of the manna was its daily appearance. Every day, Israel had enough, but not more than enough: "This is the thing which the Lord has commanded: 'Let every man gather it according to each one's need, one omer for each person, according to the number of persons; let every man take for those who are in his tent'" (Exodus 16:16). Someone has calculated that to supply an omer (about six pints) of manna for two million people daily would have required the equivalent of four freight trains of sixty cars each. God is generous and faithful. Remember, He led them into the stress of Sinai. When God leads you through difficulties, He is fully able to sustain you.

He custom tailors His provision for each day.

At the same time, He does not provide more grace than you need for your daily battles, and you are never able to set any of His provision aside for a rainy day. Moses instructed the people of Israel, "'Let no one leave any of it till morning.' Notwithstanding they did not heed Moses. But some of them left part of it until morning, and it bred worms and stank" (Exodus 16:19–20). God placed them in the position where they could not bank any of today's provision. They had to trust God every day to provide their sustenance.

God even provided a solution for the weekly Sabbath rest: "This is what the Lord has said: 'Tomorrow is a Sabbath rest, a holy Sabbath to the Lord. Bake what you will bake today, and boil what you will boil; and lay up for yourselves all that remains, to be kept until morning.' So they laid it up till morning, as Moses commanded; and [surprise!] it did not stink, nor were there any worms in it" (Exodus 16:23–24). Nothing changed in the physical makeup of the food. Banked manna didn't spoil Sunday through Friday because of its nature, but because of God's didactic purpose. He wanted Israel to learn to trust Him on a daily basis.

In the measured application of the manna we find a critical principle for the conquest of the self: God measures and individualizes the tests of our spiritual warfare. He custom tailors His provision for each day. When we see a huge test approaching, we never have a reason to be anxious. Today's grace might not be adequate for it; but when the crisis arrives tomorrow, so will the supply.

In her account of the tests she endured during World War II in a Nazi concentration camp, Corrie ten Boom recalled how as a little girl she had been frightened to learn about death. Fearful as she anticipated her parents' death, her father comforted her by asking, "Corrie, when you and I go to Amsterdam, when do I give you your ticket?"

"Why, just before we get on the train," she answered.

"Exactly," her father said, "and our wise Father in heaven knows when we're going to need things too. Don't run out ahead of Him, Corrie. When the time comes that some of us will have to die, you will look into your heart and find the strength you need—just in time."[3] He might have quoted Moses' encouragement to the tribe of Asher: "As your days, so shall your strength be" (Deuteronomy 33:25).

Sweet

Exodus 16:31 says of the manna, "The taste of it was like wafers made with honey." God did not feed Israel castor oil. In His goodness, He provided a diet that was pleasant as well as nourishing. He wanted them to "taste and see that the Lord is good" (Psalm 34:8). To feed them at all was a miracle. To feed them on food that tasted good went beyond necessity to show a personally interested love.

Supernatural

Manna was not imported from Egypt or manufactured in the wilderness. It came from heaven. It was a gift of God's grace. Jesus Christ came down from heaven, He said, to provide for hungry sinners.

Some have turned their noses up at the notion that the manna was supernaturally given. I have a book in my library that includes a photograph of a vegetable material found today in the Sinai peninsula. The picture is unhesitatingly labeled, "The Manna Israel Ate in the Desert." Apparently the author of that volume had not read Joshua 5:12, which asserts, "The manna ceased on the day after they had eaten the produce of the land; and the children of Israel no longer had manna, but they ate the food of the land of Canaan that year." Manna was supernatural food. It appeared on the ground for forty years and never again.

Visually Ordinary

For all its supernatural character, the manna was unspectacular. It did not call attention to itself by its physical appearance. It went unnoticed by Israel in the wilderness much as its counterpart, the Lord Jesus, went unrecognized by His countrymen. In fact, its name came from its unfamiliarity: "When the children of Israel saw it, they said to one another, 'What is it?' [Heb. *mahn*] For they did not know what it was. And Moses said to them, 'This is the bread which the Lord has given you to eat'" (Exodus 16:15).

Spiritual sustenance in the inner war of self-conquest is also unspectacular. God seldom provides in ways that call attention to themselves. As Israel approached the Promised Land, God stopped leading the nation through His miraculous provision of food. Likewise, the fire and cloud that had led them ceased when they reached Canaan. The change was made partly because they were no longer in one place, all headed in the same direction, and partly because of what God was attempting to do in them—to create a measure of the right sort of independence. His purpose was to mature them into people who could choose the right way because they were personally convinced of the wisdom of doing so. At Sinai, He told them what was right and wrong;

then He pointed them in the right direction. As soon as they were in the land, the cloud and the pillar of fire would have become substitutes for the personal convictions He was attempting to create.

THE SPIRITUAL MIND

The Shaper of souls has not changed His methods since Sinai. He still gives us His Word and attempts to make us people who are what Paul calls "spiritually minded": "To be spiritually minded is life and peace" (Romans 8:6). Being "spiritually minded" means being personally convinced that choosing what is right is better for me. Just as when the fire and cloud no longer appeared, God allows His children the option of making the wrong choice. Unlike Israel, we have nothing visible to lead us—only His Word and our convictions about it.

We live out a voluntary submission to God's Spirit, who speaks in the Word, because we recognize it as the only valid lifestyle. That's what the apostle implies when he says in Romans 8:7, "The carnal mind is enmity against God; for it is not subject to the law of God, nor indeed can be." The fleshly or carnal mind sees God as Someone hostile to its best interests. Being spiritually minded, by contrast, means you willingly subject yourself to God's law.

If I am spiritually minded, I am willing to take God's Word as true even when it tells me that I can do things I think I can't. When the Israelites were told to take heavily fortified cities, their first thought was to say, "We can never conquer this land." But God told them, "Yes, you can, because I will be with you and I will fight for you."

The heart ever inclines in the direction of weakness. We are always ready to appeal to our inability to do what is right. The message of Israel's wanderings is that we can do more than we think, but only if we believe Him instead of the frail groanings of our own inclinations. Immaturity says, "I can't do it." If you've ever raised a child—or even if you've been one—you know what I mean. Children will consistently try to avoid being responsible by claiming, "I can't."

I know. I tried it myself.

Until I was four, my mother and I had an understanding: She was in charge of tying my shoelaces. Then one day she dropped a bomb— I would now be expected to tie my own.

I was confused. Our arrangement had always worked so well. I couldn't see changing it, but she insisted. My response was to twist my face into an expression of agony and protest my inability to master such an exotic skill. She insisted, however, and in the end I was able, with my typically keen insight, to admit that the ability to tie one's own shoes does have advantages.

We can always do more than we think we can. Instead of building up our spiritual muscles, however, many of us act like fleas, those tiny yet trainable beasties that people sometimes teach to perform. People who engage in the training of fleas do so by putting them in a cardboard box with a top on it the exact height they want their fleas to jump. At the beginning, the fleas in the box will jump too high repeatedly and bump their tiny noggins on the top of the box. After a while, they begin to aim lower in the interests of avoiding the equivalent of a flea headache. Once the top of the box is removed, however, the fleas pose no threat to jump out because they have trained themselves to aim lower. In this respect, they resemble Christians who often settle for less than they should because they have convinced themselves they are doing as well as they can.

When we see God's Word telling us we can change, a spiritually minded person will say to himself, "God says I can; therefore, I can." Being spiritually minded means making ourselves joyfully subject to the Spirit as His will is expressed in the Word of God.

Being spiritually minded is possible because every believer has the Holy Spirit present within him. Paul explains in Romans 8:9, "But you are not in the flesh but in the Spirit, if indeed the Spirit of God dwells in you. Now if anyone does not have the Spirit of Christ, he is not His." In other words, when you belong to Christ, the Spirit of God dwells within. That is an automatic feature of conversion.

There is no middle ground with respect to the Spirit. Every living person belongs to one of two realms. We are either "in the flesh," which is the way we came out of the box; or we are "in the Spirit," which is the realm in which every believer operates. No visual clues, however, accompany the Spirit's presence. As a result, many Christians ask, "How do I know the Spirit of God dwells in me? Am I supposed to feel different?"

The testimony of God's Word, buttressed by the fruit of the Spirit (Galatians 5:22–23), ought to be enough. Being spiritually minded means accepting God's Word as true when it tells you things you can't otherwise know—such as the presence of the Holy Spirit in one's life. In Romans 8:9, that Word tells us that being a Christian and having the Holy Spirit within always go together. If you are a member of God's family, if you have trusted Christ and received Him as your Savior, then you have the Holy Spirit—whether you feel different or not.

New Life

And because we have the Holy Spirit, we have the power to make the right choices. Paul wrote: "If the Spirit of Him who raised Jesus from the dead dwells in you, He who raised Christ from the dead will also give life to your mortal bodies through His Spirit who dwells in you" (Romans 8:11). People can read this verse for years and miss its intent. Paul was not talking about a future resurrection, but a present one. We are living in bodies that are as good as dead already. They are all in the process of decay. Yet in these dead bodies that we inhabit can dwell real spiritual life. God can provide us with the power we need to please Him at any given moment. That power, like the life-giving manna of Sinai, cannot be hoarded. It must be used at the moment of choice.

The most difficult process for those of us who are Christians is keeping our hearts thirsty.

When we are faced with a moral choice, our bodies, working through that unseen principle Paul called "the flesh," will always push us in the wrong direction. But God can give life to decaying bodies by means of the Spirit. The power that raised Christ out of the grave can raise us out of our spiritual lethargy and give us the ability to do right.

Not that we always will. If we decide to do wrong, however, we have taken a step into a present experience of death: "If you live according to the flesh you will die" (Romans 8:13). Every time we do wrong, we do ourselves hurt. Rebellious Christians undergo the spiritual equivalent of leprosy. Lepers have the awful experience of seeing pieces of themselves decay and fall off as the disease advances. Spiritually speaking, when we do things that displease the Lord, we are cutting off our own members. We die just a little every time we do it. People can live for a long time with pieces falling off, but that is no way to live.

The price of doing wrong is higher than we know, for the most difficult process for those of us who are Christians is keeping our hearts thirsty. We must want to know God. We must have a longing for Him. We must long to be close to Him and please Him. When we refuse to obey, we not only have the disobedience of the moment to deal with, but we also weaken our heart's motivation. We wound that precious desire, our hunger and thirst for God, in a small way—and that desire is the greatest possession any believer has. God made us to be lovers at the deepest level of our being. His most common expression of disappointment in the Old Testament is His oft-repeated accusation that Israel was committing spiritual adultery by worshiping idols. He knew that Israel's spiritual success, as well as our own, begins when believers refuse to follow the siren song of other gods and cleave only to Him.

The Banner of the Spirit

Really living, by contrast, means taking our positions behind the Spirit: "For as many as are led by the Spirit of God, these are sons of God" (Romans 8:14). I can appreciate the way that many people use this verse, though I fear it is often applied wrong. People use the expression "being led by the Spirit" to refer to choices pertaining to their vocation or their choice of a mate or the college they attend. Those are all important choices. Christians should choose wisely in those areas. But Romans 8:14 has nothing whatever to do with decisions like that. What Paul was writing about is how the Spirit of God leads us into battle against our sinful inclinations.

Note the preceding verse's declaration that the purpose of the Spirit's leading is to help you "put to death the deeds of the body" (Romans 8:13). The apostle was not beginning a new subject in verse 14; he was still writing about inner warfare. So why did he talk about the Spirit "leading" you into self-conquest? Because without God's work, you and I would never engage in the battle. The Spirit is the only one powerful enough and righteous enough to lead us into such a conflict. The flesh will never lead us into battle against itself.

Following the Spirit also produces another benefit: Every time you put the deeds of the body to death, you show your connection with God. "As many as are led by the Spirit of God, these are sons of God" (Romans 8:14). When you see someone taking the spiritual battle seriously and consistently following his marching orders, you are looking at a person who is demonstrating his or her family connection with God.

The overcoming of ourselves in spiritual warfare is nothing less than miraculous. When we defeat a sin, it is because God has done something remarkable in us. The same power that brought Christ out of the tomb to an endless life is what it takes to lead us into battle and help us overcome those things in our lives that are displeasing to Him.

Being spiritually minded brings, as the apostle says, both life and peace. We've seen what the "life" part of the equation means, but peace also forms the product of being spiritually minded. When I am faced with a spiritual choice and I take the easy way out and do what displeases the Lord, He loves me too much to let me be happy with my behavior. Inside, I experience the guilt that my choice produces. I can never be at peace inside if I yield to the expedient rather than the right, because my conscience will remind me of my failures.

Portable Judge

The conscience has been called God's watchdog, but perhaps describing it as our own portable judge is more accurate. The conscience passes judgment on our actions and attitudes. It creates the sense of guilt we feel when we have violated our own standards of moral behavior.

Those standards do not have to be drawn from Scripture to give us pain, for conscience is a universal characteristic of human beings. Even the most remote pagan experiences guilt. God built us with an internal set of standards. Paul called it "the work of the law written in their hearts" (Romans 2:15). When we violate our internal standards, our inner being experiences turmoil, and we make ourselves vulnerable to rash and impulsive actions.

Sir Arthur Conan Doyle, author of the Sherlock Holmes stories, once chose a dozen of his socially prominent friends. To each one he sent the same unsigned telegram: "Fly at once; all is discovered." Within twenty-four hours not one of the twelve noblemen remained in the country. Doyle had no specific knowledge of any crimes they had committed, only a suspicion that his humorously intended telegram might have such an effect, and it did. The conscience always does its job.

The root of the Greek word for conscience, *suneidesis*, suggests the notion of "joint knowledge." I and my conscience both know about what I'm doing. The moral law of God is written on man's heart quite independently of anything contained in Scripture. The conscience is a traveling companion put within me by God. It exists to apply the set of moral instructions that I have accumulated through the years along with those written on my heart by God. Paul states that the conscience passes judgment on people as they "show the work of the law written in their hearts, their conscience also bearing witness, and between themselves their thoughts accusing or else excusing them" (Romans 2:15).

Western culture professes to be neutral on moral issues—even to denying that there is such a thing as a conscience—but the human spirit knows better. So do law enforcement officers. On opening day of deer hunting season, game wardens in one state placed a sign on a main road reading "Hunter Check-Station 1000 Yards Ahead." At 500 yards, the halfway point, a side road beckoned as an alternate route for guilty consciences. Lawful hunters, those who had stayed within game regulations, naturally continued on the main road. Many over-limit hunters and poachers opted for the side road—which was where the check-station really was. Whoever thought of that one should have been promoted.

Did you know that there is a Federal Conscience Fund? It exists to account for the money that people have been sending the federal government to ease their troubled consciences since 1811. The Fund has received more than three and a half million dollars, frequently accompanied by notes (often unsigned) appealing for mercy and understanding, as well as some strange communications. One supplicant submitted a money order for $125, explaining that his conscience had been keeping him awake at night. "If my conscience still bothers me," he explained, "I'll send the rest."

People have often died from the effects of their consciences. A notable example is Judas, who, crushed by the knowledge that he had betrayed such an innocent person as the Lord Jesus, took his own life (Matthew 27:3–5). Self-condemnation is so horrible that it ruins not only our ability to communicate with God, but with each other. Preservation of a pure conscience is the bottom line in the moral life of the Christian believer—a task made more complex because our consciences do not always reflect biblical standards. Sometimes they are more lax than the Scriptures; sometimes they are more severe. On occasion they choose the wrong things to be severe about, and often they are influenced more by the culture than by the Scriptures. Part of the inner war involves training the conscience to adopt divine standards rather than simply having it trained via cultural osmosis.

However it is trained, the conscience condemns not only our recent actions, but all the actions we have ever engaged in that are contrary to our own standards. This directly affects what is popularly called today self-esteem or self-image. Matters other than conscience affect our self-esteem, but by and large we either feel good about ourselves or not to the extent that our consciences have either been kept clean or violated. This is particularly important in the realm of sins of omission. It is not only the things that we do, but the things we don't do that determine how we feel about ourselves. When Paul was on trial for his life, he said, "I myself always strive to have a conscience without offense toward God and men" (Acts 24:16). A bad conscience embitters the sweetest joys; a good conscience softens the bitterest miseries.

Decisions to preserve a good conscience
must be made in advance.

When we violate our consciences, they condemn us and produce an expectation of judgment. Then when the slightest indication comes that such a judgment is near, our reaction follows—not simply to the immediate cause of our discomfort, but to all past violations. In other words, sin makes us fearful people. That is the meaning of the verse in Proverbs: "The wicked flee when no one pursues, but the righteous are bold as a lion" (28:1).

Sometimes the fleeing is quite literal. A man who was driving a truck loaded with stolen goods at night noticed a car rapidly approaching him from behind. Fearful that the vehicle would prove to be a police car, the truck driver made a radical turn to evade the "police officer" and wrecked his truck, running it into a wall. Other drivers called the police. When the authorities arrived, they quickly discovered the stolen items and the injured driver—whom they arrested.

So, what appears to be irrational flight isn't always. We react as though we have been found out, whether we have or not. God did not design us to carry around the weight of violating our core standards.

In the war of self-conquest, decisions to preserve a good conscience must be made in advance. Moral questions have to be settled without debate, for the conscience possesses two annoying characteristics.

First, it is relentless. Did you ever try to talk your conscience out of its opinion of what you just did or what you want to do? It didn't work, did it? You can never win an argument with the conscience; there is no point in trying. It is best to make up your mind from the beginning that you will lose the argument, that you will feel bad about what you have done or plan to do, and that you can go ahead and do what you are planning only if you enjoy condemning yourself.

Several years ago, a thirteen-year-old New York boy eliminated himself from the National Spelling Bee when he explained to the judges he had misspelled the word *echolalia*. They had not caught his mistake at the time. The young man explained, "I couldn't live with myself. I didn't want to feel like slime."[4] In spite of his youth, he had already learned that honesty is foundational to healthy living.

The other annoying characteristic of the human conscience is that it is powerless. The conscience does not prevent us from doing anything; it only keeps us from enjoying it after we have done it. It is a biblical presupposition that man cannot be happy and also do what is evil. Wrestling matches with the conscience are unpleasant experiences. You can never win; you can only rationalize, talking yourself into believing something you know is not true for the sake of indulging yourself.

Summarizing his own ministry late in life, Paul wrote the Corinthian believers, "For our boasting is this: the testimony of our conscience that we conducted ourselves in the world in simplicity and godly sincerity, not with fleshly wisdom but by the grace of God, and more abundantly toward you" (2 Corinthians 1:12). If you keep your conscience inviolate amid your spiritual battle, it will give you boldness in your waking hours and restful sleep at night. The Spirit leads us into battle, and the conscience confirms that our moral choices are valid as we move on our daily pilgrimage.

COURAGE

Security is mortals' chiefest enemy.[1]

—SHAKESPEARE

On October 16, 1555, a huge crowd gathered to watch the execution of Hugh Latimer and Nicholas Ridley, two bishops of the English church. Both were Reformers, converted through the influence of Martin Luther and others after they had already been in the ministry for some years. Ridley had served as personal chaplain to King Henry VIII and eventually became Bishop of Rochester during the rule of Henry's son, Edward VI. The bishop had served on the committee that drew up the first *Book of Common Prayer* for English Christians. Hugh Latimer had served as Bishop of Worcester and was arguably England's best-known preacher.

For six years after King Henry's death, Edward (aided by Protestant advisers) continued Henry's policy of making England a Protestant nation. When Edward died, however, his half sister Mary, daughter of Catherine of Aragon, came to power determined to place the English church back under the authority of Rome. Purging the church of

its Reformation-minded leaders came high on her royal agenda. Latimer and Ridley were tried on charges of heresy, found guilty, and sentenced to be burned at the stake. As the wood was ignited, Latimer
encouraged his more timid friend by saying, "Be of good cheer, Master Ridley, and play the man; for we shall this day light such a candle
in England as I trust by God's grace shall never be put out."

We rightly admire the courage that enables a faithful believer to die
cheerfully for the Lord. Courage, however, is not simply needed for dying properly; it is the indispensable weapon in the arsenal of the Christian who is engaged in living properly; in other words, in self-conquest.
Israel lacked it on more than one occasion; at Kadesh Barnea, however, the nation's cowardice cost the lives of a whole generation.

A HARD SPOT IN THE ROAD

If "Pearl Harbor" is a name that recalls treachery, "Kadesh Barnea"
should always evoke the odor of shameful surrender. On the verge of
invading Canaan, Moses sent out an intelligence-gathering group of
twelve men (one from each of the tribes) to infiltrate the Promised Land
and bring back a report. In accordance with God's direction, Moses instructed the spies,

> Go up this way into the South, and go up to the mountains, and see what
> the land is like: whether the people who dwell in it are strong or weak, few
> or many; whether the land they dwell in is good or bad; whether the cities
> they inhabit are like camps or strongholds; whether the land is rich or poor;
> and whether there are forests there or not. Be of good courage. And bring some
> of the fruit of the land. (Numbers 13:17–20)

Moses' command, "Be of good courage," was mostly ignored by
the intelligence-gathering committee. When it returned, the majority
of the group scoffed at God's promises and His faithfulness, and "gave
the children of Israel a bad report of the land which they had spied out,
saying, 'The land through which we have gone as spies is a land that
devours its inhabitants, and all the people whom we saw in it are men
of great stature'" (Numbers 13:32–33). Only Caleb and Joshua dis-

agreed, acknowledging that God was well able to make them equal to the challenges of Canaan.

What followed was a night of infamy—national self-pity rapidly followed by hostility and accusations: "All the congregation lifted up their voices and cried, and the people wept that night. And all the children of Israel complained against Moses and Aaron, and the whole congregation said to them, 'If only we had died in the land of Egypt! Or if only we had died in this wilderness!'" (Numbers 14:1–2).

Scripture records three sets of reactions to these events. The first was that of Moses and Aaron. The sacred account tells us that they "fell on their faces before all the assembly of the congregation" (Numbers 14:5). They were so humiliated by the report and the nocturnal reaction to it that they felt compelled to humble themselves before God and seek His forgiveness on behalf of such a cowardly group of people.

Timidity produces surrender
before the battle even starts.

The second reaction came from Joshua and Caleb, who tore their clothes—the traditional symbol of mourning—and issued a last-ditch appeal to the nation: "The land we passed through to spy out is an exceedingly good land. If the Lord delights in us, then He will bring us into this land and give it to us, 'a land which flows with milk and honey.' Only do not rebel against the Lord" (Numbers 14:7–9). They were grieving over the complete spiritual bankruptcy of the people who were so timid when God had given them so many reasons to be bold.

The third reaction was the most telling: God's. He considered the events of Kadesh Barnea so repulsive that He nearly took the people's lives on the spot. After an appeal from Moses, He relented, but promised: "The carcasses of you who have complained against Me shall fall in this wilderness, all of you who were numbered, according to your entire number, from twenty years old and above. . . . But your little ones, whom you said would be victims, I will bring in, and they shall know the land which you have despised" (Numbers 14:29–31).

God consigned an entire generation to wander around for thirty-eight years until they all died. Cowardice—and the stubborn disobedience that grew from its roots—had a price tag attached, and it still does. Self-conquest will go no farther than courage can take it.

What Courage Is

Courage is the willingness to fight when appearances or history tell you that you are bound to lose. The opposite of courage is timidity, the refusal to engage in a struggle deemed lost from the outset. Timidity produces surrender before the battle even starts. At Kadesh, Israel gave up before the fight and surrendered the Land of Promise to those who were already living in it.

In the spiritual battle, timidity is refusing to take on a fight with something in your life that you know shouldn't be there. It is refusing to do battle, conceding that your character and your spiritual development will stay right where they are. Behaving courageously, by contrast, means getting into the fight and refusing to be defeated. As such, it is the one indispensable weapon of self-conquest. C. S. Lewis said:

> Courage is not simply one of the virtues, but *the form of every virtue at the testing point,* which means, at the point of highest reality. A chastity or honesty or mercy which yields to danger will be chaste or honest or merciful only on conditions. Pilate was merciful till it became risky.[2]

Settling for the status quo is incompatible with self-conquest.

What Courage Isn't

Courage is not the absence of fear. In fact, courage can never exist unless your first impulse is fear, because by definition courage is overcoming your fears and fighting against what appear to be uncomfortable odds. Anybody who has made significant progress in spiritual growth has done so because he has refused to let his fears defeat him.

The more that godly people mature, the more willing they are to admit that what they find inside is frightful and intimidating. C. S. Lewis, shortly after his conversion, did a frank assessment of his spiritual life. He said, "[I] found what appalled me: a zoo of lust, a bedlam of ambitions, a nursery of fears, a harem of fondled hatreds. My name was Legion."[3] Corrie ten Boom tells how though she had suffered greatly for her faith she still was mystified at the work yet to be done in her own heart:

> It would seem, after having been a Christian for almost 80 years, that I would no longer do ugly things that need forgiving. Yet I am constantly doing things to others that cause me to have to go back and ask their forgiveness. Sometimes these are things I actually do—other times they are simply attitudes I let creep in which break the circle of God's perfect love.[4]

When I see such spiritual enemies poke their heads over the ramparts in my own life, my tendency is to surrender just because they are still there after so many years. What I need, instead, is courage; for our capacity to be courageous is our capacity to change.

LIFE WITHOUT COURAGE

When Christians refuse to challenge their shortcomings, a whole series of results ensues, none of which are good.

Nothing Is Accomplished

For starters, nothing is accomplished spiritually, because nothing is tried. The reconnaissance committee complained,

> *We are not able to go up against the people. . . . The land through which we have gone as spies is a land that devours its inhabitants, and all the people whom we saw in it are men of great stature. There we saw the giants . . . and we were like grasshoppers in our own sight, and so we were in their sight.* (Numbers 13:31–33)

Timidity leads inevitably to inability. Cowardice exaggerates problems. (It even invents them sometimes, but it almost always exaggerates them.) We can't help how big or how small we are on the outside, but because we have the Spirit of God we can choose how big we are on the inside. Unless we choose to act courageously, we will never take the risks that are necessary to change. The reference to "giants" in the people's remarks is suggestive. People who have been Christians for a long time often have tried to deal with recurring sins—their own "giants"—and have failed. If we concede the field to the giants, however, nothing is achieved.

There are no battles in a life of enslavement to sin . . . but as Paul says, it leads to death.

Southern Baptists use the name of one missionary to raise more than a hundred million dollars per year for international mission work. Lottie Moon, for whom their annual Christmas offering is named, carried the gospel of Jesus Christ to mainland China more than a hundred years ago, radically changing the dynamics of mission work. This missionary giant stood just four feet three inches tall. It would have been easier to stay home, but Lottie Moon proved to be a giant on the inside by making the effort. She refused to let her fear of failure keep her home. Christians need that sort of courage for their routine inner battles, too.

Self-Pity Rules

Where courage is missing, self-pity appears in abundance. Israel's cowardice was not exactly productive: "The congregation lifted up their voices and cried, and the people wept that night" (Numbers 14:1). The effect of their timidity is simply weeping. When people are afraid to fight, they have a tendency to direct their energies into feeling sorry for themselves. Kadesh Barnea is an incredibly ugly scene—a comedown from the kind of life Israel was supposed to lead: "If only we had died in the land of Egypt! Or if only we had died in this wilderness!" (Numbers 14:2). The self-pity that came from the Israelites' cowardice made them poor representatives of the God of heaven.

People Prefer Slavery

It was clear at Kadesh Barnea that Israel had chosen slavery over freedom. They asked, "'Why has the Lord brought us to this land to fall by the sword, that our wives and children should become victims? Would it not be better for us to return to Egypt?' So they said to one another, 'Let us select a leader and return to Egypt'" (Numbers 14:3–4). It is simpler, it is easier, to settle for a life of slavery than to be really free when courage is lacking. There are no battles in a life of enslavement to sin. All the decisions are made for you; but as Paul says, it leads to death.

The story is told of a Persian general a century ago, who used an unusual ritual in connection with executions. When a spy was captured and sentenced to death, the general offered the condemned man a choice. He could either be executed before a firing squad or suffer the undisclosed consequences that lay behind a large black door in the army's headquarters. Generally, those who were condemned chose the firing squad.

After one such execution, the general turned to his aide and observed, "They always prefer the known way to the unknown. It is characteristic of people to be afraid of the undefined. Yet, we gave him a choice."

The aide himself did not know what happened to those who chose the door, so he asked. "Freedom," replied the general, "and I've only known a few brave enough to take it."[5]

Being truly free means being liberated from debasement by your old man. Being free requires going to war to expand your freedom. Israel found it easier simply to give in and return to a place that had caused them nothing but misery. They had threatened to do so before, and with a fascinating twist of memory: "We remember the fish which we ate *freely* in Egypt, the cucumbers, the melons, the leeks, the onions, and the garlic" (Numbers 11:5, italics added). One wonders in what sense food provided by slavery could ever be considered free of charge. Israel was constantly being deceived by the false attractions of memory. They lacked courage for the fight; and when courage is lacking, no virtue can be present for long.

LIFE WITH COURAGE

Caleb and Joshua were on the Israelite intelligence committee too; but they looked at Canaan in terms of its possibilities, not its dangers.

Ground Can Be Gained

When people are courageous, ground can be gained. For Israel, it was literal ground: "Caleb quieted the people before Moses, and said, 'Let us go up at once and take possession, for we are well able to overcome it'" (Numbers 13:30). The next day, Joshua chimed in with a great line: "Only do not rebel against the Lord, nor fear the people of the land, for *they are our bread;* their protection has departed from them, and the Lord is with us. Do not fear them" (Numbers 14:9, italics added). As far as Joshua was concerned, Israel would have the Canaanites for lunch.

For us, "ground" is spiritual progress. You won't make any if you back away from the dangers. I know what it means to try and fail. It isn't fun. But in the spiritual wars you haven't really failed until you quit. C. S. Lewis said:

> No amount of falls will really undo us if we keep on picking ourselves up each time. We shall of course be very muddy and tattered children by the time we reach home. But the bathrooms are all ready, the towels put out, and the clean clothes in the airing cupboard. The only fatal thing is to lose one's temper and give it up. It is when we notice the dirt [on us] that God is most present in us; it is the very sign of His presence.[6]

Ground can be gained if you will act courageously.

Others Can Be Encouraged

Your courage will not only benefit you, but it will also move and encourage others as well. North Carolina pastor Jack Hinton, while on a short-term missions trip in Trinidad not long ago, was leading worship at a leper colony on the island of Tobago. There was time for one more song, so he asked if anyone had a request. A woman who had been facing away from the pulpit turned around.

"It was the most hideous face I had ever seen," Hinton said. "The woman's nose and ears were entirely gone. The disease had destroyed her lips as well. She lifted a fingerless hand in the air and mumbled, 'Can we sing "Count Your Many Blessings?"'"

Jack was so overwhelmed he had to leave the service. A team member followed him out and said to him, once he had gotten control of himself, "Jack, I guess you'll never be able to sing that song again."

"Yes, I will," he replied, "but I'll never sing it the same way."[7]

He had encountered a woman who simply refused to give in to self-pity. She had learned what the possibilities were when you trust God to keep your sword hand moving. Being leprous merely meant that she was deformed on the outside. Too many of us settle for being deformed on the inside.

THE WAY TO OBTAIN COURAGE

If you're a timid sort by nature, especially, how do you go about getting in touch with courage? Where do you find it? For starters, there must be a positive testimony going into your mind to oppose the constant barrage of negativism that the old man supplies. Caleb and Joshua could be so courageous because they believed God rather than their contemporaries—or their flesh. God had been saying for six hundred years that He would give Israel the Land of Promise. He told Abraham, Isaac, and Jacob in succession, "I'll give it to your descendants." In time He told Moses, "Lead these people to the Promised Land. It's time for the descendants of Abraham, Isaac, and Jacob to gain the land I promised them." He showed them how determined He was to do it by defeating the Egyptians and opening the Red Sea.

Caleb and Joshua remembered all this while the rest of the people were saying, "We'll never get it done." Caleb and Joshua said, "We'll have them for lunch. God is with us. Let's get at it." The Christian engaging in self-conquest must constantly remind himself of what the Word of God says. We must hear the possibilities.

THE WAY TO KEEP COURAGE

Remember how the apostle Paul lamented, "I delight in the law of God according to the inward man. But I see another law in my members, warring against the law of my mind, and bringing me into captivity to the law of sin" (Romans 7:22–23). Notice that phrase: "warring against the law of my mind." It is the mind that has to overcome all the negativity of the old man. We have to keep watch over what enters our minds. If we don't, after a while all the propaganda of the flesh will overwhelm us. We will knuckle under to the constant message we hear from inside us that we can never do it. Fear says, "We can never win this battle." Courage says, "God says we can. I'm going to believe God instead of my fears."

"The law of your mind" is what keeps you in the battle. The principle that provokes you and me into doing wrong, what the Bible calls the flesh, will always win unless we counteract it with what we put into our minds. Remember what Paul said, "Be transformed by the renewing of your mind" (Romans 12:2). Why do minds need to be renewed? Because the barrage of bad advice from the flesh is constant.

When the people of Israel displayed cowardice in the face of the enemy, God sentenced them to death—not instantly, but after years of meaningless activity. He did not have them die all at once. They simply went in circles for forty years. A lot of Christians are sentenced to the spiritual equivalent. Their Christian lives are marked by apathy and meaninglessness. They have a vague recollection of being excited about spiritual things once, but now it all just seems a memory. Getting into the battle will keep you sharp spiritually. You will always be on the edge, depending on the Lord, and concerned to be in partnership with Him as you take on your challenges. Being in the battle, showing courage in the battle, is the only way to live.

THE MARKS OF COWARDICE

Almost five centuries after the events of Kadesh, the psalmist penned a remarkable psalm that recalled Israel's failures there (see Psalm 95). The second half of the psalm describes the character of a heart that is both cowardly and unteachable—the exact condition that Israel found itself in. The psalmist wrote so that we might avoid the same mistakes.

Swift to Accuse the Lord

From Psalm 95:8 we discover that the cowardly heart is unteachable and quick to accuse God of bad intentions or unfaithfulness. The psalmist warned, "Do not harden your hearts, as in the rebellion, as in the day of trial in the wilderness." He is recalling the events of Kadesh when the whole nation of Israel accused God of hostile intentions merely because He had done what He had promised—brought them to the edge of Canaan. Somehow, they had absorbed the devilish thought that God only leads people into pleasant experiences.

Fanny Crosby, the writer of many of the best-loved lyrics in Christian hymnals, was only six weeks old when a physician placed an incorrect poultice on her eyes and she became permanently blind. In spite of her disability, when Fanny was eight years old she made a decision that would affect her entire life. She did not ask God for anything material or to make her able to see, make her smart, make a wonderful man fall in love with her, or help her become rich or popular or famous. She simply asked God for a way to serve Him.

Her prayers were answered. She was able to attend a fine college for the blind. She met and married a songwriter. Because of the quality of her poetry, she was in time invited to Washington where she addressed the Congress of the United States. Though she had written many songs, when she was forty-four someone suggested that she consider adding to her work the composition of sacred songs and hymns.

The suggestion proved to be a turning point in her life as she wrote many of her now famous hymns of praise—more than eight thousand of them, in fact, in her life of ninety-five years. Her output includes "All the Way My Savior Leads Me," "Blessed Assurance," "I Am Thine, O Lord," "Jesus is Tenderly Calling," and "Jesus, Keep Me Near the Cross."

Fanny Crosby harbored no bitterness against the physician and obviously none against God. In fact, she once said of the doctor, "If I could meet him now, I would say thank you, over and over again, for making me blind." She felt that her blindness was a gift from God to help her write the hymns that flowed from her pen. According to those who knew her, Miss Crosby probably would have refused treatment even if it could have assured the restoration of her sight. A Christian who is attempting to plant God's flag over the unwon portions of his or her inner life won't be inclined to point an accusing finger toward heaven—or toward people, for that matter.

Slow to Remember God

The insubordinate and cowardly heart also has a nasty tendency to forget what God has already done for it. Israel certainly did: "Your fathers tested Me; they tried Me, *though they saw My work*" (Psalm 95:9, italics added). The Israelites in the wilderness put God to the test, even though they had seen His work repeatedly on their behalf. They were a nation of slaves who had been brought together, made a cohesive people again, given a reason to live, rescued from the Red Sea and Pharaoh's army, given food to eat and water to drink in the wilderness—and their attitude toward God was, "What have You done for me lately?"

Stubborn in Response to God

When you find a person who will not bend under God's pressure, it may be the result of the worst of all spiritual diseases: stiffening of the neck. The worst feature of stubbornness is that people often don't recover from it. Instead of having a malleable spirit like that of Fanny Crosby, an unteachable person often proves so resistant that he makes spiritual change impossible and exposes his folly for the whole world to see.

One need only review the Exodus narrative to be convinced. There you see a pharaoh who not only lost a national resource (the Hebrews), but who was seen to be a fool in the process. Why? Because stubbornness and unteachability in the Scriptures almost always go together; they form the twin products of unbelief. Settling into an attitude of anger against God yields unspeakable follies. It forgets God's past kindness altogether.

Psalm 95:7 provides the divine prescription: "If you will hear His voice." The psalmist says in effect, "You will never get anywhere spiritually until you realize that what God has given to us in this book is His very voice. He didn't write these things as a historical curiosity; He wrote them as His enduring invitation to any who have settled into a stubborn attitude toward Himself."

The writer to the Hebrews, using Kadesh Barnea as the heart of his chapters 3 and 4, insists that the key word in Psalm 95 is "Today." "Today, if you will hear His voice" (Hebrews 4:7). God is speaking, appealing to the one inclined to be stubborn. His appeal is for change *today.*

THE EFFECTS OF COWARDICE

A whole generation died from their timidity in the wilderness. God had tolerated a great deal of disappointing behavior from Israel, but when they refused to fight for what He had promised they could not lose, that was too much.

Disgust

If we need any other reasons to turn away from the stubborn and cowardly behavior of Israel, they appear in Psalm 95:10–11, where the psalmist explains where stubbornness leads. God said, "For forty years I was grieved with that generation." The word grieved means "disgusted." Some have translated it, "I loathed that generation." Nothing repels God more than a Christian who has every reason in the world to bow the knee and resolutely refuses to do so. It disgusts Him.

Can God be disgusted with a Christian? Certainly. He can feel about His children the same way we do about our own. Their behavior can provoke and even horrify us, though we have an undying commitment to their welfare. His disgust is purely a temporal matter, but it is nevertheless real. And what provokes it is His finding in us a stubborn refusal to acknowledge our sins and move in a new direction.

Wandering

Refusing to be taught may well produce an aimlessness in life. God described Israel at Kadesh as "a people who go astray in their hearts" (Psalm 95:10). Since they went astray internally, God consigned them to roam externally. Israel wandered in the wilderness for forty years. The people's physical wandering was an expression of the fact that in their hearts they were aimless. When you become a stubborn individual, you are telling God that you don't want His leadership. The results of that may be an aimless, boring life. Unfortunately, many churches are filled with people who match that description.

Ignorance

God summarized the stubbornness of Israel by the description, "They do not know My ways" (Psalm 95:10). When you reject God's ways, you are on your own. That is a heavy penalty, because the world is a complex and dangerous place to navigate without God.

Whether our hearts are filled with panic or with insubordination, the results are the same. There may be matters in your life that God has been speaking to you about in His Word for years. Are you listening? Do you hear His voice in the Word of God? Are you afraid to submit your will to His? The alternative is unthinkable. As the psalmist points out, we are His sheep. We were made to follow. The only question is, "Whom will we follow?"

CHAPTER SEVEN

DEFEAT

[No] created thing, shall be able
to separate us from the love of God
which is in Christ Jesus our Lord.
—ROMANS 8:39

Christians struggle with failure. Many seem to think that God has no place on His team for losers. They live in a state of denial concerning personal problems, using the approach taken by the college football coach who had struggled with several losing teams. He explained, "When you're about to get run out of town, get out in front of the crowd and make it look like you're leading a parade."

We seem unwilling to be vulnerable to people, as though the world will only judge our message valid if our lives are trouble free. Christian musicians, for example, often receive pressure from record companies to omit references to real-life hardships in their music. Michael Card wrote a song about the suicidal tendencies he experienced as a college student. "It took me four or five years of processing to finally write a song about it," he said. Marketing executives were deeply alarmed by the song's message and thought he should not publish it. According to Card, they said, "People do not want to perceive that Michael Card struggled with suicide. This is bad for your career."[1]

Nothing in Scripture, however, suggests that Christians should deny that they have had or are currently having struggles. The Bible makes no attempt either to deny or hide the blunders of the people of God. David's great catastrophes are well known, as are Peter's denials. Elijah's timidity before Jezebel is chronicled as frankly as Jonah's indifference to the welfare of Nineveh's multitudes. For sheer numbers, however, Israel in the wilderness wins the prize.

Israel's following of the Lord changed dramatically between the heady days of Egypt and the crushing disasters of the Sinai. When Moses went through his series of confrontations of Pharaoh, miracles were the order of the day. All challenges to the people of God were crushed. The Israelites in Egypt had seen four centuries of slavery and misery, but from the time God set out to redeem them, they knew a nearly continual series of successes. Then, as they stepped onto the road to true freedom, they met failure after failure.

God had not changed His mind about them, of course. He knew what He was getting before He ever sent Moses back into Egypt. Nor had He changed the rules in the middle of the game. He was merely attempting to bring Israel out of a kind of national spiritual infancy to maturity; and when God undertakes to do that, the people who are the objects of His love often find themselves confused.

What causes the confusion is our failure to see that Christian growth is not a one-size-fits-all suit. God tailors the experiences that confront us to fit our spiritual condition. In the early days of Christian living, we often know the exhilarating successes that the nation of Israel experienced as it left Egypt; every day brings a new demonstration of God's power and grace.

Later, however, we begin to experience failure. The amazing providences of our youth seem to disappear; the euphoria that accompanied our original knowledge that we were part of the family of God has subsided; the answers to prayer that we had known daily now are less frequent.

What has really happened, of course, is that we have been promoted. God has moved us into a more challenging course of spiritual development because He knows that we are now able to bear it. We find ourselves in the position of Paul's disciples in Asia. As he and Barnabas made their initial visits to that Roman province, they preached the gospel and saw many conversions. Then they made a second trip through those same communities bearing a different message for the people who had already believed. They went about "strengthening the souls of the disciples, exhorting them to continue in the faith, and saying, 'We must through many tribulations enter the kingdom of God'" (Acts 14:22).

In the process of strengthening disciples, God never loads more on us than we can handle. When Paul described the value of studying the great story of Israel's Exodus and Conquest, he made this very point: "No temptation has overtaken you except such as is common to man; but God is faithful, who will not allow you to be tempted beyond what you are able, but with the temptation will also make the way of escape, that you may be able to bear it" (1 Corinthians 10:13).

When the people of Israel encountered an increase in troubles in their travels through the Sinai wilderness, they were merely experiencing what was ordinary and to be expected as they progressed toward God's promise. Their thirst and discomfort did not indicate that God was less interested in them, but that He was teaching them dependence on Him.

Growth is a painful business, yet there is no alternative. When children coo and gurgle in their cribs, they are truly adorable, but they are also deficient in several ways. Parents can enjoy them thoroughly at this stage of life, but part of the joy is knowing that the time will come when they will be out of the crib and able to converse with their parents and enter into their lives in more meaningful ways. Just because we enjoy infants does not mean we want them to remain so, still less that we want them, at some later time, to desire to be infants again.

Yet Christians often look back on the days after conversion just that way. They remember how it was, and they want it to be that way again, but it will not happen. Like it or not, God intends for us to experience the thousand natural shocks that make up human experience with all the spiritual challenges they bring. When we fail, as we will, the solution is not to long to be spiritual infants again. In any case, God loves us too much to allow that.

Nor are we to collapse spiritually and declare our own case hopeless, citing as evidence the painful experiences we have recently known. Rather we should continue to walk, placing one foot in front of the other, in joyous recognition that we have passed out of babyhood and are now deemed worthy to experience the challenges of our maturing state. God can transform the pains of failure for our good as we increasingly sense our inadequacy and are drawn to cling to Him more closely. As the apostle Paul noted, nothing—not even our own sins—fall outside the scope of God's good purpose for us: "*All things* work together for good to those who love God, to those who are called according to His purpose" (Romans 8:28, italics added). We are not to sin that good may come, but God can use our defeats as well as our victories.

The biblical descriptions of God as a Rock, a Fortress, a Deliverer, and the like all reinforce the discovery that we find hard to swallow: We are weak people. I don't like to think of myself that way, and I am sure you don't. After all, I grew up in America, where self-reliance and independence are treasured virtues. Four decades of spiritual growth, however, have had their effects. God has at last convinced me—though I am sure I will need to be reminded—that I cannot possibly meet the demands of warfare against the world, the devil, and even my own old man apart from His help. The job is simply too big for me, as my blunders prove. I feel at times like the novice ship's captain who was learning to navigate Chesapeake Bay with its innumerable rocks, sand bars, and shoals. He asked a veteran skipper how he learned to avoid such dangers. The answer was short and to the point: "I hit 'em all."

For many of us, driving out our innate confidence in ourselves is the first order of business for God as He takes us through our personal wilderness. Such an objective cannot be met while we live in comfort. He sees to it that we walk toward the kingdom of God; but between here and there we will go through many a dry wilderness and know the heartache of disappointing Him and others. What our dry experiences should not do is to cast doubts on the reality of our original entry point into Christian living. The generation of Israel that was already destined to perish because of Kadesh Barnea discovered that just a few miles down the road.

A FAMOUS INTRODUCTION

If you were to ask a hundred Christians at random, "What is the most familiar verse in the Bible?" chances are good that most would pick John 3:16, where Jesus says to Nicodemus: "For God so loved the world that He gave His only begotten Son, that whoever believes in Him should not perish but have everlasting life." Indeed, the passage may have been the direct cause of the conversion of more people than any other text in Scripture. For example, in the introductory pages to the Bibles found in hotel rooms and public buildings all over the world, John 3:16 can be found in several dozen languages. In a sense, the verse is a condensation of the entire Bible.

But were you to ask, "What statement introduces John 3:16?" you would probably receive a lot of blank looks. At the risk of getting personal, do you know the answer without looking? (OK, "John 3:14–15" is the right answer; but what does that passage *say?*)

Jesus was speaking to Nicodemus, a religious but unconverted man, providing an illustration of what God's saving grace is all about: "As Moses lifted up the serpent in the wilderness, even so must the Son of Man be lifted up, that whoever believes in Him should not perish but have eternal life" (John 3:14–15).

"As Moses lifted up the serpent in the wilderness."

Doesn't sound *that* profound, does it? But it is. In fact, that little word *as* addresses one of the most significant issues of Christian experience: Can I be certain of my standing with God even when my war of self-conquest is going badly?

Indeed, inner warfare can prove so discouraging at times that people begin to doubt whether God could have pardoned someone with such problems. John 3:14 touches directly on the question by taking us back to an event in the wilderness wanderings of Israel. Not long after Kadesh Barnea, the people of Israel again repeated their familiar complaint: "Why have you brought us up out of Egypt to die in the wilderness? For there is no food and no water, and our soul loathes this worthless bread" (Numbers 21:5).

God had performed miracle after miracle to get them to this place. Every morning when they rose, their breakfast was lying on the ground. All they had to do was walk out and collect it. Their enemies' bones and chariots were being washed by the salty waters of the Red Sea. Yet they complained about their treatment. To top it off, these were the people who already had heard judgment pronounced against them. The adults knew they would never see the Promised Land because of their unbelief, and still they exhibited more.

In spite of their precarious condition, the doomed nation had just received a wonderful answer to prayer before their outburst of complaining. The Canaanite king of Arad had attacked the Israelite column and taken prisoners, causing great consternation. The nation was so distressed that it placed itself under a vow, pledging to God, "If You will indeed deliver this people into my hand, then I will utterly destroy their cities" (Numbers 21:2). The Lord then proceeded to do precisely what they asked. He was active in working with them in spite of their own disappointing behavior.

After this victory, however, the nation had to make a long detour around Edom, because God did not want them fighting with their Edomite relatives. On the long walk, the people became discouraged and began to complain, issuing their indictments against God and Moses, complaining about the scarcity of water and the limited menu (Numbers 21:5). God's gift of manna they construed as valueless, even though their lives depended on it.

THE CURE

God's reaction was both just and revealing: "The Lord sent fiery serpents among the people, and they bit the people; and many of the people of Israel died" (Numbers 21:6). It appears that the poison of the serpents was a comparatively slow-acting one, although uniformly lethal. The time lapse between the bite and death set the stage for the importance of the episode and the feature that Jesus used to explain salvation to Nicodemus. The Lord's use of *as* ("*As* Moses lifted up the serpent . . .") provides the key. Jesus' own death on the cross, the cure for sin, would in time prove analogous to the cure provided by the serpent in the wilderness. The parallels are revealing.

Initiated by Grace

For starters, God didn't have to provide a solution at all. He could have let Israel's offenders die. They deserved no better; in fact, he had already sentenced them to die. Yet He chose to provide a solution out of

His grace. And what an interesting solution! A snake hanging on a piece of wood: "Make a fiery serpent, and set it on a pole; and it shall be that everyone who is bitten, when he looks at it, shall live" (Numbers 21:8).

Mankind, likewise, deserves no better than to suffer the eternal effects of his own indifference to God. Paul explained, "As it is written: "There is none righteous, no, not one; there is none who understands; there is none who seeks after God. They have all turned aside; they have together become unprofitable; there is none who does good, no, not one" (Romans 3:10–12). Yet God in grace, as in the wilderness, has provided a solution in Jesus Christ who, like the serpent, was displayed publicly as the object of a saving look.

Designed for the Condemned

Those who were bitten by the serpents were as good as dead when the bite took place, though they may have lingered on for a while. After the bites, their bodies contained all that was necessary to effect their deaths.

Man brought sin into the world,
and Man took it away.

Mankind, in the same way, has already received its just sentence of death from God. Now humans merely await the inevitable. It is one of the great victories of satanic theology in the world that people think they must do something particularly heinous to merit eternal punishment. Not so, said the Lord Jesus: "He who does not believe is condemned already" (John 3:18). The rejection of the truth God provides about Himself is all the justification God needs to condemn (see Romans 1:18–23).

Conveyed by Good News

People who were bitten by the serpents were in all stages of discomfort. Some, newly bitten, may have experienced nothing more than an immediate stinging sensation and some swelling around the wound. Others, who had received their bites earlier, may have been unable to move and hovering near death. Because the camp was so large, someone would have had to relay the word that God had responded favorably to Moses' prayer and had provided a means of survival. Everything depended on the victims' reaction to that news. Some would have had to be helped into a position where they could see the bronze serpent. Others could have walked. Some might have continued sitting in their tents; in other words, they might have done nothing. But if any person believed the news about God's cure, he could go and look at the bronze serpent. That was all he had to do. God asked for no promises. There were no guarantees that once a bitten Israelite had looked he would not return to his objectionable behavior. All God required was a look.

Linked to the Cause

Why would the Lord Jesus liken Himself to a snake? Because the snake was the symbol of both the problem and the solution. The serpents were symbolic of sin. The people rebelled, and their sin rose up and bit them. They were dead people; it was just a matter of time. And they deserved no better, as they admit: "We have sinned, for we have spoken against the Lord and against you; pray to the Lord that He take away the serpents from us" (Numbers 21:7).

The Lord Jesus came to earth to become sin for us. He became the last Adam, living among us as a human being. Man brought sin into the world, and Man took it away. As He hung on the cross, the sin of the world was poured out on Him. Paul explains in 2 Corinthians 5:21, "He made Him who knew no sin to be sin for us, that we might become the righteousness of God in Him." The organism that brought death also brought life.

Instantaneous

For those who looked at that serpent, the issue was settled instantaneously. All that was required was a look at the serpent on the pole: "Everyone who is bitten, when he looks at it, shall live" (Numbers

21:8). The moment the look took place, the problem was solved. Whether the swelling went down immediately or subsided gradually didn't matter. It was just a matter of time. Those who looked were cured, and cured completely.

The very simplicity of this requirement may have kept some from taking advantage of it. They might have thought, as some do of the good news of the gospel, that to fix one's hopes of life itself on the work of someone else was silly. There must be something more to it than that. But those who thought so perished.

Permanent

God's cure was also permanent. The one who looked only had to look once. He did not have to return to the pole every day and look again. The cure was as permanent as the injury was deadly. Still, I imagine there were some who awakened the day after their cure wondering if it was still valid. Some of them may even have gone back to the serpent to look a second time, or a third time.

Was there anything wrong with looking a second time? No, but the one who went back repeatedly was suggesting by his actions that the terms of God's solution couldn't be entirely trusted. The returnee was attempting to split the responsibility with God, instead of just believing what God had said and letting it rest there.

Similarly, untold numbers of people have never quite been able to rest in the completed work of Jesus Christ. They keep returning and attempting to confirm through their own actions what they have been told. I once heard of a man, for example, who had been baptized thirteen times, including every conceivable form of the ritual. He had been baptized by immersion, by sprinkling, by pouring, by immersion three times forward, and by immersion three times backward. One of them had to be right, he figured, and he wasn't taking any chances. His actions betray a restlessness that should not be present in one who has fixed his trust in the finished work of Christ. Some people continue to respond to invitations on Sundays, or try to "pray through" or seek emotional validation of their faith in various ways. However, if I have trusted in Christ, I can know that He has saved me. Faith in Christ is much like faith in a physician; I either trust him or I don't. The transaction that takes place when I put my trust in Christ needs no more confirmation than my own realization that He is trustworthy.

There is an old hymn that isn't sung much any more, but that captures the truth of Numbers 21 decisively. It says,

> There is life in a look at the Crucified One,
> There is life at this moment for thee;
> Then look, sinner, look unto Him and be saved,
> Unto Him who was nailed to the tree.

The power of Jesus' illustration of the serpent is reinforced by its context. John 3:14 formed part of the same conversation in which Jesus told Nicodemus that he had to be born again (John 3:3, 5). Like the look at the serpent, birth is also not reversible. We can't lose our family relationship by anything we do after we are born. Even if we misbehave and our parents disown us, that doesn't change the fact that we are related to them. We may not share in the enjoyment of their wealth, but nobody can pass legislation that changes the consequences of physical birth. Once born, always born. Once alive from the dead, you are alive eternally.

THE DIFFICULTIES

For some, Jesus' illustration raises lots of questions. It flies in the face of everything that we are trained to believe. All our lives we are taught that what is truly valuable must be earned by our efforts.

Human Nature

Human nature finds that grace freely expressed is hard to deal with. But consider this: If the Lord Jesus in fact paid all our debt of sin so that one act of faith is all that is required, do you think that God would want us to know that? Or would He want to hide that information from us? Would He keep such information from us in order to provoke godly living? In other words, would He prefer to motivate us by (a) a consciousness of the possibility of impending doom, or (b) a conviction about the permanence of His love?

If you are a parent, you will understand this similar question: Are you threatened when your children have a strong conviction that you love them? Are you afraid that that knowledge will lead them to take advantage of you? Or do you think it is healthier for them to doubt in some measure that you truly love them? Would it benefit them to think that they could do something so bad that you would stop loving them altogether?

In one of his books, Charles Ryrie tells about how in his younger days he worked with underprivileged junior high and senior high kids in his hometown. From time to time, the leaders of the Bible clubs these young people were in would reward those who had achieved some special goals with an overnight trip to a camp in the country.

On one occasion, he remembers, he was the leader of a group in one of the camp cabins. It was a Friday night—actually the wee hours of Saturday morning—and he was awakened by a noise to find that several of his group leaders had gotten out of bed, gone down to the lake, found a boat, rowed far out from shore, and were having a gleeful time in midlake.

Of course, this behavior broke every statute in the camp rule book and was quite dangerous besides. Ryrie went to the water's edge and motioned for the offenders to return. When they arrived, he told them to go back to bed and that he would decide in the morning what their punishment would be.

Grace attaches no strings.

It was Charles Ryrie who spent a sleepless night, however, because he couldn't decide what to do. To make the decision more complex, he had just taught the preceding afternoon on the concept of grace: that God freely loves and freely forgives. So he endured a nocturnal debate with the Lord. He kept considering whether he should come down hard on his campers, and the more he thought about it, the more he remembered how the Lord had dealt with him. In addition, the youngsters had not been shown much grace in their lifetimes. His mental "argument" proceeded like this:

> *But, Lord, I can't forgive them; they don't deserve it.*
> Neither did I.
> *But, Lord, I have to enforce the rules.*
> I'm glad, Lord, You didn't.
> *But, Lord, if I'm too kind, the kids will think I'm weak.*
> I never thought You were weak, only loving.
> *But, Lord, first I'll make them promise never to do something like this again, and then I'll forgive them.*
> It's a good thing You didn't require that of me, or I never would have been forgiven.

The next morning Ryrie called them together and told them that he had forgiven them, no strings attached. They thought he was kidding and kept saying, "There has to be a catch." He explained that he was trying to show them what the grace of God was all about. He even did the cabin chores all that day to keep any of them from thinking that they could earn what he had extended freely.

He recalls that as long as those young people were in his Bible club they were the epitome of goodness, helpfulness, and usefulness. They never presumed on the grace he extended them.[2]

Human nature is always looking for the catch. Grace attaches no strings.

Superficial Logic

A superficial logic says this: "If you believe in the permanence of salvation, you will fall into sin and live as you please." Yet untold numbers of people have lived in holy faithfulness to God who did believe it. Living as you please is not a necessary consequence of believing in the permanence of salvation. Indeed, it is not even a likely consequence for those who appreciate both the vastness of God's holiness and His love.

Of course, some people who believe in it do fall into sin. But so do a lot of people who don't believe in it. People fall into sin for reasons that have nothing to do with what the Bible teaches about the permanence of salvation.

When we are children, often our behavior is dictated by our fear of what our actions may do to us. As toddlers, if we grow up with godly parents, we learn to fear the rod. As time passes, we become more concerned with the consequences of our actions on our own hopes and ambitions.

When we become adults, however, an important shift takes place. We become concerned less with what our actions may do to ourselves and more with what they may do to people we love.

When I first went to college and was living away from home, I was faced with a lot of new temptations—the same ones young adults everywhere face. I was saved from many a destructive and foolish act simply by thinking about what it might do to my mother to hear of my follies. I wasn't afraid of what she might do to me, but I was concerned about the pain I might cause her.

Such is a proper and valid concern for a Christian engaging in the war of self-conquest. Our failures are a source of grief to God and ought to be avoided: "Do not grieve the Holy Spirit of God." We should not grieve Him because "by [Him] you were sealed for the day of redemption" (Ephesians 4:30). We strive to avoid grieving the Lord not simply because of what He might do to us, but *because of the irreversibility of what He already has done for us.*

I remember the first time I was aboard a Boeing 747 jumbo jet. I forget our destination, but I do remember being impressed with the size of the airplane—especially its weight, which runs in the neighborhood of two hundred tons fully loaded (as we were that day). We began to move slowly down the runway. We rolled . . . and rolled . . . and rolled. It seemed that we would never become airborne. A couple of passengers down the aisle from me decided that they wanted to help, so with a smile they pulled their feet off the floor.

A lot of Christians are like that. They believe that Christ has saved them, yet they want to add to what He did, just in case; but nothing can be added, or needs to be:

I need no other argument,
I need no other plea;

It is enough that Jesus died,
And that He died for me.[3]

Going into battle with the old man is important; but much of its importance lies in the fact that <u>the Christian soldier fights fully equipped for battle</u>: enabled by the power of God, sustained by the love of God, and made secure by the righteousness and justice of God.

CHAPTER EIGHT

COMMUNICATIONS

For the word of God is living and powerful,
and sharper than any two-edged sword.
—HEBREWS 4:12

Joshua cautiously moved through the trees alongside the river, allowing the morning fog to obscure his movement. He wanted to get a good view of Jericho, the immediate objective of his army. The people of the city had retreated inside the walls some days ago, but caution would serve him well nonetheless. The town, enclosed inside heavily fortified walls and strategically placed near the only road that led into the hill country, posed a challenging battle problem. How should the army approach Jericho's fortifications?

He remembered the town from his scouting expedition thirty-eight years before, a time when he and eleven others had been sent out by Moses to reconnoiter the land. The scouting party, with the exception of himself and his good friend Caleb ben-Jephunneh, had panicked at the sight of those formidable walls. The group's pessimistic intelligence report, made in spite of God's assurances that they could defeat the Canaanites, had crushed the morale of the army.

The episode had proven to be the last straw in Yahweh's dealings with that generation. He had decreed that all the adults that had left Egypt would die in the wilderness on account of their stubbornness and unbelief. Though God had said that Israel could not lose the war, the scouts had insisted that they could not win—and the people had succumbed to the scouts' evaluation. Now it was the new generation's turn to face Jericho and the other walled cities; and Joshua, as their leader, was still uncertain how to undertake the process.

A slight noise to Joshua's left sent a chill to the back of his neck. He turned to see a dark shape moving toward him in the mist: a warrior with a drawn sword. Had the people of Jericho stationed sentries near the river after all? He unsheathed his own sword and issued a challenge.

"Are you for us or for our adversaries?"

The reply was as thrilling as it was unexpected: "Neither. I am the Commander of Yahweh's army!"

Joshua's response epitomized the stance of the Christian warrior; he "fell on his face to the earth and worshiped, and said to Him, 'What does my Lord say to His servant?'" (Joshua 5:14).

When a battle must be fought against an entrenched enemy, the Commander must command. His Word can vanquish any foe. For that reason, meditation and prayer hold the honored places at the top of the list of weapons for waging internal warfare. Actually, we could simply say "meditation," for meditation—properly understood—includes prayer. Nothing in the believer's arsenal can compare to meditation for spiritual effectiveness. Nothing is so masterfully designed by God to do the believer good.

Unfortunately, this pivotal tool for interior reconstruction is poorly understood today. In fact, I find that a great many Christians are fearful of "meditating," for they consider it to be a practice welded to eastern religion and the New Age Movement. After writing a book on meditation,[1] I did a series of radio and TV interviews on the subject. The first question on nearly every occasion was, "How does what you are advocating in your book differ from Eastern or transcendental meditation?" Clearly, Eastern religion has managed to persuade people that the origins of meditation lie in Hindu and New Age thought.

Only an era with shallow biblical roots could entertain such a suggestion, however. Meditation is mentioned as early as the book of Genesis (24:63). Later, the psalmist referred to it as his regular activity, called on believers to practice it daily (Psalm 1:2), and wrote the longest chapter in the Bible about it (Psalm 119). Something with such pivotal importance and ancient roots ought to be the focus of a great deal of Christian energy. So tell me: When was the last time you heard of a conference on biblical meditation? I'm still waiting to be invited to my first one. By ignoring or downplaying this crucial issue, Christians helped create a void into which the Beatles and the Maharishi Mahesh Yogi came rushing in 1969. Ever since, advocates of Eastern religion have been pushing "meditation" as the leading edge of their misguided theology.

The mind-numbing routines of Eastern religion have nothing to do with biblical meditation, however. Meditation as described in the Bible involves filling the mind with the Scriptures, then pondering God's truth, personalizing it, and responding to it in worship and obedience. God's truth cuts into the inner person in ways that are amazingly effective: "The word of God is living and powerful, and sharper than any two-edged sword, piercing even to the division of soul and spirit, and of joints and marrow, and is a discerner of the thoughts and intents of the heart" (Hebrews 4:12). The more our inner lives are exposed to the Scriptures, the more we are equipped to put to death those attitudes and actions that displease the Lord. One thing we can be sure of: When we engage in biblical meditation we are majoring on the majors. When we meditate, God will use His Word to accomplish His goals in and through us.

Joshua found out for himself what meditation could do from an authoritative Source. Imagine for a moment the challenge this man faced after Moses' death. Israel's late leader was certainly a tough act to follow, and even he had found it a difficult task to keep the people pointed in a healthy direction. By the time he died, however, Moses was so highly regarded that God made a point of dispatching an angel to bury him (Jude 9). The funeral took place in a remote location that was soon lost, or else someone soon would have come and built a shrine over it.

What with all the rebels and malcontents in the ranks, Joshua must have been more than a little nervous about his new appointment as

Moses' successor. As he was contemplating his coming challenges, God came to him at the Jordan and gave him the key to his future success. As the Angel of the Lord, He urged him to carry on, adding this caution: "Be strong and very courageous, that you may observe to do according to all the law which Moses My servant commanded you; do not turn from it to the right hand or to the left, that you may prosper wherever you go" (Joshua 1:7). Success in any endeavor—leading Israel into the Promised Land, building a business, or pastoring a church—God linked to keeping in touch with His truth. And how was Joshua to do this? The succeeding verse explains: "This Book of the Law shall not depart from your mouth, but you shall meditate in it day and night, that you may observe to do according to all that is written in it. For then you will make your way prosperous, and then you will have good success" (Joshua 1:8).

Joshua's task was ostensibly military and administrative, not purely religious. His job was to take Israel into the land God had promised. On the surface it might have seemed that he needed analytical and strategic expertise above all. God exploded such a notion by telling him that he first needed to be the right sort of person. God can make a godly person into a successful general simply by being present with him: "Have I not commanded you? Be strong and of good courage; do not be afraid, nor be dismayed, for the Lord your God is with you wherever you go" (Joshua 1:9).

THE PRACTICALITY OF PRAYER

Joshua would have had many an occasion to put that promise to the test and call on God for protection and strength. At the same time, many of his prayers would have grown from his practice of meditation on God's truth. The two go together.

In Psalm 119, the psalmist penned an exquisitely beautiful prayer about the Scriptures. The psalm makes reference to the Word of God in almost all of its 176 verses, which are arranged in twenty-two stanzas of eight verses each. Psalm 119 forms the longest prayer in the Bible, and it expresses the heart of a person who is engaged in an all-out war against what is improper in his life: "My soul breaks with longing for Your judgments at all times" (Psalm 119:20). That is the statement of a man who has been developing his inner life for years. If we are honest, most of us will have to admit that we don't always feel that way about the Word of God. Few of us engage God in prayer on such a level. Do our hearts long supremely to have such a command of His Word that it will constantly judge our actions and keep us pure before Him?

The specific requests in Psalm 119 surprise us, too. For example, the psalmist asks God for clear vision as he peruses the text of Scripture: "Open my eyes, that I may see wondrous things from Your law" (Psalm 119:18). Apparently, simply opening the Bible and starting to read is not enough to draw from God's law all the sustenance and beauty to be found there. If God does not open our eyes, we will miss much of what we need.

The psalmist prays as well that God will not hide His commandments from him: "I am a stranger in the earth; do not hide Your commandments from me" (Psalm 119:19). Why would he pray for something like that? Would God hide His commandments from a believer? Isn't He concerned to make His Word known to everyone?

God *is* concerned to make His Word known; but the Bible is different from every other book in one critical respect: the moral prerequisite for interacting with it. You can understand and profit from other books regardless of the state of your heart—but not the Scriptures. God routinely hides His commandments from those who have no intention of dealing honestly with them.

We may have a copy of the Bible that we can read, but God's commandments will not really be ours until we are disposed to obey them. God knows whether we want to know His truth in order to deal with it, or just to impress others. If He discovers insincerity in us, He indeed will hide His commandments from us. We may have the Book, but the Book will not have us. The psalmist in effect prayed, "Lord, I'm like a foreigner in this land. I don't know my way through the complexities of life. I need direction, and You're the only One who can provide it. Don't hide Your road map from me." As people who are just passing through this world, we need the guidance that God's truth can give us—but we must really want His help.

Does your prayer life run along such lines? I don't mean to take anything away from intercessory prayer; it is both important and commanded in Scripture. When you look at the prayers of the Bible, however, a large percentage of them—and the book of Psalms provides the best examples—seem to be occupied with one person's soul and its spiritual growth. The Psalms serve as a severe rebuke to us much of the time, for we often reduce prayer to a tool for solving what we regard as "practical" problems: help with paying the bills, protection for the missionaries, concerns about our health, and the like.

The psalmist prayed about practical matters, too, but his definition of what was practical cast a wider net. Nothing is more practical than to pray for a connection with God's truth. He knew that enormous challenges faced him and that above all he needed to become the right sort of person in order to come to grips with them.

*Often our prayers are anemic
until they are sufficiently desperate.*

Prayer has a direct application to the spiritual battle, of course. When doing battle with the old man, we often encounter hard pockets of resistance in our lives. Wisdom dictates that we cry out to God when we find ourselves failing to gain consistent victories in a given area.

But what happens when we ask God for help, go into battle, and then fail again? When the pattern repeats itself, we easily slide into the erroneous conclusion that God never intended for us to defeat a given problem. What are we to make of it when we ask God over and over again for help—and He seems not to come to our aid? C. S. Lewis said,

> You must ask for God's help. Even when you have done so, it may seem to you for a long time that no help, or less help than you need, is being given. Never mind. After each failure, ask forgiveness, pick yourself up, and try again. Very often what God first helps us towards is not the virtue itself but just this power of always trying again. For however important

chastity (or courage, or truthfulness, or any other virtue) may be, this process trains us in habits of the soul which are more important still. It cures our illusions about ourselves and teaches us to depend on God. We learn, on the one hand, that we cannot trust ourselves even in our best moments, and, on the other, that we need not despair even in our worst, for our failures are forgiven. The only fatal thing is to sit down content with anything less than perfection.[2]

The spiritual battle often involves two not always compatible goals. On the one hand, God wants us to win. On the other, however, He wants us to understand the completeness of our need of Him. Of the two, the second is harder to learn. Often our prayers are anemic until they are sufficiently desperate. And prayer is only part of the answer.

THE MECHANICS OF MEDITATION

God's presence and approval are linked in the prayer here (and elsewhere) to meditation on God's truth. Putting enemies to death—whether physical enemies like the Canaanites or spiritual ones like the sins in our lives—works best when we draw near to the Source of ultimate power. We, like Joshua and David, do well to meditate on God's truth day and night.

J. I. Packer defines meditation as

the activity of calling to mind, and thinking over, and dwelling on, and applying to oneself, the various things that one knows about the works and ways and purposes and promises of God. It is an activity of holy thought, consciously performed in the presence of God, under the eye of God, by the help of God, as a means of communication with God. Its purpose is to clear one's mental and spiritual vision of God, and to let His truth make its full and proper impact on one's mind and heart. It is a matter of talking to oneself about God and oneself; it is, indeed, often a matter of arguing with oneself, reasoning oneself out of moods of doubt and unbelief into a clear apprehension of God's power and grace.[3]

The Scriptures form the essential subject matter of meditation. The psalmist wrote, "Oh, how I love Your law! It is my meditation all the day" (Psalm 119:97). The first and second parts of that verse are closely connected. If we love God's law, we will want to place it in the forefront of our mind as often as we can. It is useful to think of meditation as a four-step process.

Realize God's Truth

First comes understanding that truth, and that involves reading and study. I don't have to understand every detail and implication of a passage to benefit from it, but I do need to understand its basic assertions and assumptions. Simply reading the text does little good for my inner person unless I grasp what God is saying in it on two levels. I must ask (1) *What did this mean to the original readers?* When Paul wrote to the Ephesians, those Christians in Ephesus were the original beneficiaries of what he had to say. After satisfying that question, however, I must proceed to ask (2) *What does this mean for today . . . for me?* The local application of Paul's words to the Ephesians simply forms a pattern into which we look to discover the timeless character of God and His ways.

The "realization" step is the place to use Bible study tools: concordances, dictionaries, and the like. My goal is to understand what God was saying through the human author to the original readers— and by analogy to me.

Realizing God's truth is only the first step in meditation, but that is as far as most people get. The only reason to read and study God's Word, however, is to engage in the last three steps.

Retain God's Truth

The second step in meditation is retaining God's truth. By that I mean memorization, or at least a degree of immersion in the text that will approximate memorization.

Is it possible to meditate without memorizing? Yes, but only if you have the text open in front of you. For that reason, it is impossible to "meditate day and night" (a phrase that appears a number of times in Scripture) without memorizing.

If we are going to take the Word along with us mentally, then we will be inclined in most cases to memorize only a verse or two. Most people can memorize one verse (or even part of a verse) to think about as the day progresses. An expression like, "Be anxious for nothing" (Philippians 4:6), the opening phrase of a much longer sentence, can provide all the spiritual fodder we need for several days. The goal here is not to prepare for a memory contest but to expose our hearts to God's truth in a deeply personal way. We don't need to retain the passage for recitation years from now, though we may in fact be able to do that in many cases. The purpose is to have it in our consciousness long enough for it to do God's supernatural work of reshaping our values. A by-product of daily memorization is that much of what we memorize for a day *will* stay with us for years, or even for a lifetime: "Your word I have hidden in my heart, that I might not sin against You" (Psalm 119:11). Once His Word is "hidden" inside us, we can move to the third step.

Reflect on God's Truth

Step three in meditation is reflecting on what you now understand. The primary Hebrew word for meditation means to utter a low, nearly inaudible sound (it is used of the cooing of a dove). The term suggests becoming so occupied in thought with the features of the biblical text that words spring spontaneously to the lips. That partly explains the otherwise surprising reference made in Joshua 1:8: "This Book of the Law shall not depart from your mouth." We might have expected "This Book of the Law shall not depart from your mind" or "your heart." Reflection is where we become genuinely *involved* with the text . . . even to the point of "thinking out loud" about it.

Recalling how God rescued me from uncertain situations in the past ought to alleviate, or at least ease, my anxieties.

Take that brief excerpt of Philippians 4:6 I mentioned a moment ago. As I reflect on it, I might ask myself: "Have I been worrying about anything lately? Have I been taking on responsibility for outcomes that properly belong to God? Have I created anxieties for myself by procrastinating in some area of life? What areas of my experience repeatedly cause me to become an anxious person?" In mulling over issues such as these we find ourselves walking in the steps of the psalmist, who said, "I thought about my ways, and turned my feet to Your testimonies" (Psalm 119:59).

As a consequence of my answers, I might remind myself of God's past mercies and His faithfulness in an attempt to quiet my anxious heart. David wrote, "I remember the days of old; I meditate on all Your works" (Psalm 143:5). Recalling how God rescued me from uncertain situations in the past ought to alleviate, or at least ease, my anxieties.

Respond to God's Truth

The fourth and final step in meditation is responding to the truth of God and the implications for my behavior and values that have emerged from step three. Responding will often mean (before anything else) obedience. It will also usually involve prayer in some form; the exact nature of the response will often be dictated by the text itself. To take our example (Philippians 4:6) a step further, I might, as I consider how I have behaved or thought, acknowledge my failings in the area of anxiety. I might well have to admit to God that I have been behaving and thinking as if everything depended on me.

Or I might have to confess that I have no confidence in my ability to keep my anxieties under control: "Lord, I really need Your help in this area. When I read my Bible, I see how You are in charge and how You make even the weakest of people able to meet their challenges. Thank You that You can do that for me too."

Should my text for the day include a statement of blessing, my response would be correspondingly different. For example, I might read Romans 5:8, which says, "God demonstrates His own love toward us, in that while we were still sinners, Christ died for us." My prayer might be, "Lord, thank You for loving me when I was unable to appreciate it. Help me be a channel of Your love by loving, for Your sake, someone who is lost." A natural sequel to that prayer might be to make a list of people who need to know Christ and to begin to build bridges of God's love to them. If, on the other hand, I read the account of David's sin with Bathsheba, I might ask God to help me keep my eyes where they belong so that I do nothing to dishonor Him. The response portion of meditation is often implicit in the nature of the biblical text itself.

As you can see from this brief introduction to the subject, there is nothing especially exotic about meditation. It requires no Hebrew or Greek or even great literary ability. The central issue with meditation is loving the Word and recognizing it for what it is: God's gift to me to help me know Him better. If we see it the way we should, at some point we will begin to understand the psalmist's "breaking soul" (Psalm 119:20). A person who yearns for the Scriptures will go to the trouble to learn those judgments and personalize them. He will turn violations of God's commands into confessions, the commands themselves into appeals for help, the blessings of the Word into thanksgivings, and the promises of the Word into personal hopes. He will, in effect, do what the psalmist did—allow the Scriptures to form the music of his inner being: "Your statutes have been my songs in the house of my pilgrimage" (Psalm 119:54).

Prayer and meditation will make us the right sort of people. As we interact with the truth that penetrates deep into our inner being, we are going to be challenged, rebuked, encouraged, and provoked to do things differently. We need both to reshape our belief system and our values and to tell God how we feel at each step along the way. If we're doing well, we can tell Him that. If we're struggling, we can tell Him that, too. Prayer and meditation together is how the Bible becomes *our* book instead of just a book.

That raises the question of how to develop the kind of hunger for God's Word that we see (for example) in the psalmist's words in Psalm 119. The starting point for most of us is interacting with the Scriptures and with their Author when we have less than a breaking soul. Sometimes we simply have to start our prayer and meditation on the basis that we know it is what we should do—in other words, out of a sense of duty.

That is true of much of the spiritual battle. We engage in activities because we know we need to, not because we possess a burning enthusiasm about them. What we see in Psalm 119 reveals the psalmist's heart after he had become enthusiastic for God's truth; but nobody, including David, starts that way. The flesh is too strong in us. One writer says:

> You can feel the hostility of the flesh whenever you approach God—it makes real love for him into work: Digging around in the Bible to find a juicy new insight to impress your small group is like sailing the Caribbean, but poring over the Scriptures to find the Lover of your soul is like skiing *up* Mount Everest. Conjuring up a happy mood with some music you don't even know the words to is like solving 2 + 2 with a calculator. But savoring the glory of Christ and his tender love until your heart is softened toward him is like using mental math to calculate *pi* to the thousandth place.[4]

The key is continuing to do it out of duty long enough so that you see and become excited about what God is doing in you through that dutiful obedience. When that happens, you, like the psalmist, will be thrilled with the prospect of interacting with His Word in prayer and meditation, and your life will show the difference.

C H A P T E R   N I N E

SECRETS

*We can have no fellowship with the enemies of
God within us or around us, but to our hurt;
therefore our only wisdom is to maintain
unceasing war against them.*[1]
—MATTHEW HENRY

John Donne, though better known as an outstanding English poet
of the seventeenth century, was a pastor by vocation. When Donne
was a young and somewhat wayward believer, he endured many un-
happy moments as he fought the battle of who would have control of
his life. Finally yielding to Christ, he determined to offer himself for
whatever use the Master wanted to make of him. After receiving his
training and being ordained in 1615, he was assigned to preach in the
parish of Keyston, Hunts.

When he arrived in Keyston, he walked into the churchyard and
noticed the sexton digging a grave. He walked over to introduce himself just as the man discovered a skull. As the two struck up a conversation, the sexton handed the newly discovered artifact to the pastor
for his inspection. As Donne was pondering the skull, he noticed that
a headless nail, barely observable, was lodged in its temple; he extracted
it (unseen by the sexton) and wrapped it in his handkerchief.

The pastor asked the sexton if he knew whose skull they were handling. The man replied that it had been that of a local saloon keeper who had died in bed after a night of drinking.

"Had he a wife?"

"Yes."

"Is she living?"

"Yes."

"What character does she bear?"

"A very good one; only her neighbors reflect on her because she married the day after her husband was buried." The response raised troubling thoughts in Donne's mind; he determined that at the appropriate time he would call on the woman and explore the matter.

When he did, the woman explained that her husband had died from excessive drink, but Pastor Donne noticed that her conversation was troubled and uneasy. In the midst of her somewhat evasive explanation, he pulled the handkerchief from his pocket and asked, "Do you know this nail?" Horrified at the sight of what she thought was (literally) buried and hidden, she burst into tears and confessed the murder of her husband.

Normal humanity cannot bear guilty secrets painlessly for long. Those who make the attempt may appear to others to be functioning well, but their spiritual nerves lie close to the surface and it takes only a touch to bring out the hurt and the consequences once again—as Israel discovered after the victory at Jericho. The tragic events occurred at a place called Ai.

THE WRONG TIME TO PRAY

To introduce the episode, here's a quick and practical test of your Bible knowledge: When did God find it necessary to rebuke a godly man for praying? Are you stumped? It happened three times, all on Israel's journey to the Promised Land. The first time, God told Moses to stop praying and get the people moving through the Red Sea (Exodus 14:15). Sometimes praying can get in the way of obedience, and when unpleasant or risky work is waiting to be done, more praying about it will not help.

The second rebuke also was directed at Moses. Apparently, he kept praying that the Lord would allow him to enter the Promised Land even after God had said it would not happen. Moses later told his countrymen, "The Lord was angry with me on your account, and would not listen to me. So the Lord said to me: 'Enough of that! Speak no more to Me of this matter'" (Deuteronomy 3:26).

We generally learn more in defeat than in victory.

On the third occasion, Joshua was the individual concerned. God's rebuke was even more severe than with Moses, and resulted from the sorrowful episode at Ai (Joshua 7).

As places went, Ai certainly was one. In fact, the word "Ai" simply means "a ruin" or "a pile of rubble." One wonders about the chamber of commerce that would give such a name to its hometown. I have heard of Rockville, Rockford, and Rockport. I have even heard of Rock City (though I haven't seen it). But pity the poor people who, when asked for the location of their home, had to say, "I live over in Rockpile."

Ai was so forgettable, in fact, that its exact location has passed into the mists of history.[2] Nobody knows exactly where Ai was, and it may be just as well, because the events that transpired there contributed a bitter memory to the people of God.

However, though Ai can be forgotten, the lessons from it should not be. We generally learn more in defeat than in victory, and for that reason a review of the events of Ai can be useful as an example of what not to do in the process of self-conquest—and as a help in knowing when not to pray. The defeat at Ai happened because Israel had been keeping a guilty secret since the battle of Jericho, though only one family in Israel knew it at the time. Joshua had explained to the nation prior to the battle that the entire city of Jericho would have to be destroyed. The valuable items of gold and silver to be found there would be dedicated to the treasury of the tabernacle of the Lord and were off-limits for Israelite soldiers. As far as the nation was concerned, those items were accursed.

Unfortunately, an Israelite named Achan disobeyed God's instructions and took some of the restricted items for himself and secreted them in his tent. In doing so, he unwittingly set a trap for the nation that resulted in the defeat at Ai: "The children of Israel committed a trespass regarding the accursed things, for Achan . . . took of the accursed things; so the anger of the Lord burned against the children of Israel" (Joshua 7:1).

Though Achan served as the primary culprit, his complacent countrymen compounded the problem. After the enormous victory at Jericho, Israel was riding high. The next objective on General Joshua's list turned out to be this much smaller town called Ai, located in the hills above the now-smoldering remains of Jericho. When a scouting party sent out by Joshua returned, the contempt in their voices was unmistakable: "Do not let all the people go up, but let about two or three thousand men go up and attack Ai. Do not weary all the people there, for the people of Ai are few" (Joshua 7:3).

Israel chose not to take the battle seriously because the opponent seemed unimpressive. Because Israel was harboring a guilty secret, however, Ai's power against the nation was magnified. The Lord had withdrawn His protection because Israel had not maintained its national integrity.

The results were crushing:

So about three thousand men went up there from the people, but they fled before the men of Ai. And the men of Ai struck down about thirty-six men, for they chased them from before the gate as far as Shebarim, and struck them down on the descent; therefore the hearts of the people melted and became like water. (Joshua 7:5)

It is hard to resist the notion that Israel was just a little cocky because it had enjoyed an essentially effortless victory.

The Israelites had 635,000 foot soldiers, and they used three thousand against Ai. When they finished, thirty-six people were dead, and 635,000 were demoralized. They drew unwarranted conclusions from their victory at Jericho, somehow inferring that all their battles would resemble the walkover they had just experienced. They were wrong. Spiritual warfare is hard.

Which brings us back to Joshua's rebuke. The great leader had called a prayer meeting after his nation's terrible defeat. He and the elders of Israel were feeling the pain of humiliation intensely and personally. They spent the rest of the day on their faces at the tabernacle, with dust on their heads and dismay in their hearts (see Joshua 7:6). There can be no question about their sincerity. The Lord listened to their prayers and their musings about God's reputation and finally said to Joshua, "Get up! Why do you lie thus on your face? Israel has sinned, and they have also transgressed My covenant which I commanded them. For they have even taken some of the accursed things, and have both stolen and deceived; and they have also put it among their own stuff" (Joshua 7:10–11). God, of course, was unconcerned for His wealth; He was disturbed because of Israel's spiritual poverty.

Joshua, unaware of the sin in the camp, was proceeding as though relations between the nation and the Lord were normal, and they weren't. God and Israel weren't on speaking terms because of Achan's secret sins. Israel was praying for blessing when there was unconfessed sin in the camp, and God had decided that it would have to be rooted out: "You shall be brought according to your tribes. And it shall be that the tribe which the Lord takes shall come according to families; and the family which the Lord takes shall come by households; and the household which the Lord takes shall come man by man" (Joshua 7:14). The guilty party would then have to be executed (v. 15).

STAGES OF DESCENT

When all the lots were cast and Achan was designated as the guilty person, he finally revealed the sad story of how he had brought Israel into defeat and placed his own life in jeopardy:

Indeed I have sinned against the Lord God of Israel, and this is what I have done: When I saw among the spoils a beautiful Babylonian garment, two hundred shekels of silver, and a wedge of gold weighing fifty shekels, I coveted them and took them. And there they are, hidden in the earth in the midst of my tent, with the silver under it. (Joshua 7:20–21)

His words describe four stages of descent into the defeat at Ai. Because of these steps into darkness, the nation had been embarrassed and demoralized—to say nothing of the thirty-six deaths in combat that could be laid directly at his feet.

Seeing

Achan first saw the goods: "I saw among the spoils" (Joshua 7:21). At this point, the problem could have been easily handled. He could have simply looked away. It was the second glance that started the downward spiral.

Sin works that way. We cannot always avoid the presentation of an opportunity to sin. We *can* keep our eyes from fondling the opportunity. As Martin Luther often said, "You can't keep birds from flying around your head, but you can keep them from building a nest in your hair."

Coveting

The second step downward took place deep inside Achan: "I coveted them" (Joshua 7:21). The Tenth Commandment was designed by God to keep overt sin at arm's length. This sordid episode hung on Achan's inattention to it and to his inner lack of contentment. God's faithfulness in feeding him and taking care of his family was ignored. When we are not content with what God provides, we open ourselves to self-destructive longings.

Taking

"I coveted them and took them" (Joshua 7:21). Lust is the driving force that results in the next step, overt sin. The way to deal with sin is to face it at the level of desire, before it results in wrong actions. Deal with it in the heart, and it will be manageable. Wait until it has a grip on you, and it becomes unmanageable. It became a monster to Achan and caused him to steal things that belonged to God.

Hiding

Once Achan had stolen the goods, the next step was to hide his sins. The cover-up is the final and most damaging stage in the process. He fell for the lies that coveting had presented. For all his troubles, he had a Babylonian garment that he couldn't use (someone would certainly have recognized it as part of the Jericho booty) and some gold and silver that he would have to hide for some time. By entertaining the temptation, he had lost his capacity to think clearly. At this point, the loop of temptation was complete: "Each one is tempted when he is drawn away by his own desires and enticed. Then, when desire has conceived, it gives birth to sin; and sin, when it is full-grown, brings forth death" (James 1:14–15).

*The way to avoid divine discipline
is to beat God to the punch.*

Everybody else had also suffered because of the cover-up, so it had to come to an end. God prescribed an elaborate process of uncovering Achan's folly. Israel came by tribes; then the selected tribe came by clans; the selected clan came by families, the families by individuals. Why go to this trouble? God could have told Joshua about the problem directly.

Apparently God did not do so in order to give Achan time to confess the offense on his own. When his tribe was chosen, he might have been debating the wisdom of confessing his sins. When his clan was chosen, he must have felt God's perfect knowledge closing the net. However, he allowed the process to work all the way out. It was only when God pointed the finger directly at him that he confessed. There is no great virtue in confessing one's sins when there is no alternative.

This elaborate process directed at uncovering Achan reinforces the principle given by the apostle Paul: "If we would judge ourselves, we would not be judged" (1 Corinthians 11:31). The way to avoid divine discipline is to beat God to the punch. God is patient. He will wait awhile for us to deal with secret issues ourselves. But He will eventually deal with them if we don't.

He dealt with them severely in Achan's case:

Joshua, and all Israel with him, took Achan the son of Zerah, the silver, the garment, the wedge of gold, his sons, his daughters, . . . and all that he had, and they brought them to the Valley of Achor. And Joshua said, "Why have you troubled us? The Lord will trouble you this day." So all Israel stoned him with stones; and they burned them with fire after they had stoned them with stones. (Joshua 7:24–25)

They even named the place "Achor" ("Trouble") because of what happened there.

At first consideration, we wonder about the severity of Achan's treatment. Why so harsh? And why were the children involved? Not long before Ai, Moses had given Israel God's safeguard for national justice: "Fathers shall not be put to death for their children, nor shall children be put to death for their fathers; a person shall be put to death for his own sin" (Deuteronomy 24:16). The fact that family members were executed means that we can be sure that Achan's wife and children were involved in the cover-up. Indeed, how could they not have been? The goods were hidden in the family tent (Joshua 7:22), something they would have known. They said nothing and in their tacit inactivity joined the guilt-covering conspiracy.

THE MILITANT CHRISTIAN'S CLEANSING PROCESS

Achan's hiding of his sin was nothing new in human experience. Ever since Eden, humanity has been honing its skills of evasion and buck-passing. On that fateful day when sin entered human life, the man blamed the woman and the woman blamed the serpent. Adam even blamed God by implication, by accusing "the woman whom *You* gave to be with me" (Genesis 3:12, italics added).

Even people who have great spiritual advantages can fall in the blunder of shunning responsibility. A classic case took place at the base of Mount Sinai when Moses discovered that Aaron had fashioned a golden calf for Israel to worship. When called to account for himself, Aaron explained to Moses:

Do not let the anger of my lord become hot. You know the people, that they are set on evil. For they said to me, "Make us gods that shall go before us."

. . . And I said to them, "Whoever has any gold, let them break it off." So they gave it to me, and I cast it into the fire, and this calf came out. (Exodus 32:22–24)

Sure it did, Aaron.

The first impulses in human history after man's initial rebellion were guilt and the evasion of responsibility. The Christian who engages in self-conquest will need to understand both these matters and know how to deal with them.

Self-conquest will always collapse unless it operates on the basis of reality: "Behold, You desire truth in the inward parts, and in the hidden part You will make me to know wisdom" (Psalm 51:6). That integrity that God desires in the inner person must be maintained as we do battle with the old man. As we meditate on God's Word (see chapter 8), we are constantly being exposed to the light of His truth. That light keeps our relationship with God healthy: "If we walk in the light as He is in the light, we have fellowship with one another, and the blood of Jesus Christ His Son cleanses us from all sin" (1 John 1:7). The Christian life is always to be lived in full exposure to the brilliant light of God's truth.

When that light calls a sin in my life to my attention, I am faced with a choice: Will I acknowledge it or shut my spiritual eyes and refuse to face it for what it is? The apostle John describes what happens when I take the second option: "If we say that we have no sin, we deceive ourselves, and the truth is not in us" (1 John 1:8). The ultimate deception is self-deception, and that is practiced by the Christian believer who refuses to face the reality of sin in his life. He does more than simply tolerate an impediment to an open relationship with God, he steps into darkness. He is no longer walking in the light.

The alternative is confession, the open acknowledgment to God— and to others if they have been injured—that we have been wrong. John explains, "If we confess our sins, He is faithful and just to forgive us our sins, and to cleanse us from all unrighteousness" (1 John 1:9). Trying to keep our sins secret destroys our inner integrity, mars our fellowship with God, and, because we are walking in darkness, makes our spiritual progress unpredictable.

Some have sought to invalidate the importance of confession by saying that Christians should never seek what they already have (for-giveness of sins). While superficially plausible, the objection fails on several points. To begin with, John includes himself in the pronoun: "If *we* confess our sins . . ." The apostle needed to confess his own sins from time to time, as every Christian does.

John first heard of the necessity of confession from Jesus Himself, who taught His followers to pray, "Forgive us our sins, for we also for-give everyone who is indebted to us" (Luke 11:4). This appeal does not negate the reality of the legal accomplishments of the Cross. A judge in family court might fine his son for speeding and even pay the fine himself; but when father and son arrive at home, the father will ex-pect his son to take steps to lay the personal issue to rest. Family dis-cipline does not deny the reality of an unbreakable tie between family members; indeed, it is built upon that tie. We will never answer at God's Great White Throne for the sins we confess daily, but that is no rea-son to sin. A strong relationship with God is built on obedience and upon honesty at those times when we have sinned. The militant be-liever harbors no guilty secrets before God.

John's statement about confession addresses two critical problems of restoration to fellowship. He first notes that God is *faithful* to for-give us; we can count on His forgiveness when we confess our sins. This wonderful statement addresses His commitment to maintain a rela-tionship with a person who has violated His will. Knowing of God's faithfulness encourages us when we feel the guilt that comes from do-ing wrong. We are sometimes prone to wonder whether what we have done can be forgiven. John's statement in 1 John 1:9 assures us that it can.

He also points out that "He is . . . *just* to forgive us" (1 John 1:9, italics added). God's forgiveness does not compromise His holiness. The sins He forgives have been paid for by the blood of Christ (1 John 1:7; 2:2). Most English translations render 1 John 1:9, "He is faithful and just to forgive us our sins," though the word *our* does not appear in the original text. John did not use the possessive pronoun, only the article. We might translate it literally, "He is faithful and just to forgive us *the* sins." The particular sins in view, of course, are those we con-fess. When we confess, we acknowledge the sins we know about, and God forgives those.

He goes farther, however, and also forgives those of which we are unaware: "and to cleanse us from *all* unrighteousness" (1 John 1:9, italics added). His cleansing covers everything that would separate us from the full enjoyment of fellowship with Him. We scarcely know the degree to which we fail to conform to God's perfect holiness . . . which is a mark of His grace. If we knew it, chances are good we would be crushed by it. He knows, but that knowledge creates no barrier between us as long as we confess what we do know about.

God does not ask that we walk *according* to the light, however, but that we walk *in* it (see 1 John 1:7). If God required perfect behavior before He allowed us to enjoy His fellowship, no one would enjoy it. As it is, He asks that we continually expose ourselves to the light of His Word, and as we do so He reveals to us in His time the faults that are properly the object of self-conquest.

As long as we respond when we see our sins and acknowledge them before Him, our fellowship continues unbroken. The moment we refuse to do so, we are repeating the deadly blunder of Achor, and we have left the brilliantly lighted path that God Himself walks (1 John 1:5). While we function in the world, we do well to remember that progress in the work of self-conquest is built on the reality of God's knowledge of us: "There is no creature hidden from His sight, but all things are naked and open to the eyes of Him to whom we must give account" (Hebrews 4:13). The more clearly we see ourselves in the light of His Word, the more open and valuable our communication with Him will become.

ADVANCE

The meaning of earthly existence lies, not as
we have grown used to thinking, in prospering,
but in the development of the soul.[1]
—ALEKSANDR SOLZHENITSYN

The soullessness of the Western world these days is unwittingly crystallized at a theme park in Anaheim, California, called Tinseltown Studios. At Tinseltown, people get to experience celebrity—for a fee of forty-five dollars. The glamour begins when the ticket holder is escorted down a red carpet to the cheers of an adoring crowd hired for the occasion. "Fans" crowd around, demanding the autograph of the newly crowned celebrity. Paparazzi feverishly compete for pictures. Every few feet, a new television crew stops the "celebrity" and requests an interview.

Then the person enters an auditorium filled with gorgeous models, each desperate to have pictures taken with such an august personage. At dinner, celebrities-for-a-night watch the new videos of themselves with their adoring fans. They can even (for an additional fee) go to an editing room and have themselves digitally edited into a scene from a famous movie. The "audience" then votes on the best performance. Winners are called on stage to receive their "awards," and if they find themselves speechless, Tinseltown provides them with prepared acceptance speeches.

Apparently, for some the experience is exhilarating. One acting student gave her opinion: "Walking up on the carpet, all these people coming up to you and treating you like you're in the movies—that's our dream."[2]

Celebrity without achievement does appear to be the dream of many people—a sad and pathetic one, even if it is in keeping with the theme of the age: "Image is everything." Unfortunately, Christians can be caught up in such mirages as easily as anyone else.

However, believers will find greater fulfillment by pointing themselves toward a life that can be approved by Jesus Christ. If we are so approved, worldly accolades will take their proper place. However, we will never advance in the spiritual realm without recognizing that spiritual achievement can't be had for a forty-five dollar fee; it comes from a patient and believing application of the weapons of spiritual warfare.

One of those key weapons is faith. By faith I refer not primarily to the trust that brings salvation; that transaction of faith is merely what gets us onto the battlefield. Only converted people are qualified to engage in self-conquest. The faith I have in mind refers to the thousands of occasions after conversion in which we are called on to believe God and trust Him for our daily challenges and temptations.

Before Israel entered Canaan, God said to Joshua, "Every place that the sole of your foot will tread upon I have given you, as I said to Moses" (Joshua 1:3). God said, "I have given it to you already." God's statement was contrary to what Joshua saw with his physical eyes. As he gazed across the Jordan, he saw a country with dozens of cities, heavily fortified, occupied by belligerent peoples. The ground had yet to be won.

Yet God said, "I have given it to you." He even put it in the past tense, as if to emphasize that it was simply a matter of time and obedience. And even though Joshua had yet to win a foot of ground, God encouraged him and Israel with His promise of being with the people as they fought.

FAITH: MYTH AND REALITY

We are to meet all of our own challenges to growth with faith, believing that God will be with us in the fight and that we will certainly win if we simply keep at it. Spiritual warfare cannot be waged without faith. Unfortunately, even the idea of faith is very poorly understood today and subject to a number of myths.

Myth #1: Faith Is a Kind of Self-Hypnosis

A lot of people feel that the job of the Christian is to talk himself into believing something that, deep down, he is quite unsure about. If he can do so, he consequently pumps himself up into a highly emotional state so that he can sail through the challenges of his life. The underlying inference is that truly spiritual people live in a state of denial about the harsh realities of life in the world, and that is what keeps them going. That, however, is a myth.

The reality is quite different. Faith is not self-hypnosis; it is a series of individual transactions, each of which we must meet by answering a question. The question is addressed by God to us and is always the same: "You see what I say in My Word about this. Are you going to believe Me, or not?"

Most of the spiritual people I know are hardheaded realists. They are hardly in denial. They know that the realities of life call for a lot more than a positive mental outlook. Trying to pump up one's emotions rarely works, for emotions are not causes; they are effects.

Faith is confidence in what another has said.

God's challenge/promise to Joshua about the land laid the onus on Joshua and Israel. They would now have to live each day by putting their feet all over the territory God had promised them. Their sandals became symbolic of whether they were believing God or not. Of course, there were people already in the land who were not about to yield it easily. Faith would be exercised when the soldiers of Israel strapped on their weapons and moved in the direction of the enemy. Courage is energized by faith, but every threat requires a new transaction.

Myth #2: Intensity Creates Outcomes

A second myth asserts that the strength of a believer's faith determines the outcome of whatever is pending. To transport this myth into Joshua's situation: If Joshua believed God intensely, Israel would win its battles. If he wavered, Israel would lose. But this, too, is a myth.

Faith is absolute. You either have it or you don't. If you have the weakest faith in the strongest ice, you are in no more danger of falling through it than if your confidence in it is absolute. The ice determines the outcome, not the faith. The faith only has to do with my enjoying the outcome.

People even talk about "false faith" as though there were such a thing. There is faith in what is false, but the expression "false faith" is nonsensical. It is like talking about a circular square. Faith by definition is knowledge and the confidence that grows from that knowledge. If you have faith, you have confidence. To say someone has a false faith is to say that they have an untrusting trust.

Faith is confidence in what another has said. It is not, at its root, a religious word. You and I have faith every day in what people tell us, and we behave in ways that display our faith. The moment a doctor prescribes medicine for me, I come to grips with an issue of faith: Will I trust his or her competence and good intentions, or not? Few patients go to the trouble of investigating their physicians' degrees and medical training, and even those who do so are merely shifting the focus of their faith to the word of a medical school.

Life is filled with demands for faith; it is hardly the province of the intellectually challenged or the spiritually gifted. If I have my brakes fixed by a mechanic, getting in the car and driving expresses my faith. My action says that I believe what my mechanic told me: that he fixed my brakes. I am willing to risk my life on that, because I don't really think it is a risk at all. I have confidence in my mechanic. But please note: My faith will not change anything about what happens to me. If he didn't fix my brakes, my faith in him won't make them work.

If Joshua simply did what God said and fought the battles before him every day, in time he would look around and see no more enemies. The same principle is true in the inner battle (though the final victory will not come until the old man no longer exists).

The important thing about faith is exercising it moment by moment. My success has nothing to do with the intensity of my faith. It has everything to do with the competence of the One in whom I rest my confidence.

Myth #3: Faith Starts with What I Want

The third myth about faith is that I am the crucial person in my faith. That is, I decide what I want to believe God for, and from that point the critical issue is how strong my faith is. "I'm believing God for enough money to pay off my mortgage" is an example. Another: "My wife is unconverted, but I'm believing God for her salvation." These statements make sense only if God had said something about the satisfaction of the mortgage or the conversion of the person's wife. In Scripture, however, God issues no promises about specific mortgages or the conversion of particular individuals. Faith does not begin by my pulling out of the air what I want to happen. I cannot say, "I'm believing God that my addiction to alcohol will be conquered by May 1" and expect that my statement will somehow settle the issue.

The reality is that faith starts with God and ends with my reaction to what He has said. Faith is my response to God's revelation. If God hasn't said anything, I have nothing to believe.

To return to the previous example: I do know that God has said something about the conversion of a mate. In 1 Corinthians, God cautions Christians who are married to unbelievers this way: "If the unbeliever departs, let him depart; a brother or a sister is not under bondage in such cases. . . . For how do you know, O wife, whether you will save your husband? Or how do you know, O husband, whether you will save your wife?" (7:15–16). So God explicitly says that no believer can be sure about the eventual conversion of his mate. Maybe it will happen, maybe it won't. God has not said in His Word that certain individuals are exceptions. So "believing God for a mate's conversion" is not something that Christians can do. When the mate dies unconverted, does that mean God lied about it? Of course not. If God has said it, I ought to believe it. If He hasn't said it, then it might or might not happen.

One can, of course, be hopeful, using the means available to contribute to a mate's conversion: prayer and conversation. But making up an outcome and then "believing God for it" falls outside the biblical idea of faith.

We believe God only when we get into the fight against those enemies.

As Israel approached Canaan, Joshua was operating within the realm of what God had said. God had told him that if he took the army into battle, in due course Israel would win the land. Joshua didn't invent something to believe. God had spoken.

FAITH AND SELF-CONQUEST

What do you think the average Israelite soldier thought when it came time to cross the Jordan and go into battle? I'm sure that there was a mixture of excitement, fear, and anticipation. Some people must have gone into battle in a very excited state. Others may have been dreading it. So who believed God? Who in Israel exercised faith?

The answer is "Every person who went into battle." The ones who didn't believe God were those who didn't march with the army. People hiding in the tents were the people who didn't believe. Those who placed the soles of their feet on the new ground were exercising faith. God had said He would give them victories, and *they believed Him enough to fight.* For Joshua and his army, faith was what got them into the struggle.

And what about us?

Self-conquest works the same way. God has said in His Word that there are matters in our lives that are our enemies and His:

The works of the flesh are evident, which are: adultery, fornication, uncleanness, lewdness, idolatry, sorcery, hatred, contentions, jealousies, outbursts of wrath, selfish ambitions, dissensions, heresies, envy, murders, drunkenness, revelries, and the like. (Galatians 5:19–21)

This is just one list, but probably there are a few things on it that we have to admit we are guilty of from time to time.

Conquest of the self involves replacing those items with the corresponding virtues that follow: "love, joy, peace, longsuffering, kindness, goodness, faithfulness, gentleness, self-control" (Galatians 5:22–23). Even the most mature believer will admit that God gives us ample scope for doing battle. The more we grow in our knowledge of Him, the more we see the many ways that our lives need to be more Christlike, and the more we become conscious of the sins that still remain a part of us.

We believe God only when we get into the fight against those enemies. When you open your Bible and something you read points out a fault in your life, that is a divine challenge to get into the fight. The enemy, our flesh, opposes all such efforts. The Canaanites were sure they could whip Israel. They had everything going for them, or so they thought. They knew the land better than Israel. They had proven warriors. They were behind the gates of fortified cities. They were ready to counterattack. But the Canaanites lost the land, for the weakest faith in the God of great promises will produce miracles; and the Christian life is one unending miracle. The believer fights his battles as one alive from the grave (see Romans 8:11).

MIRACLE AT GIBEON

Focusing on the challenges of Christian living, as I have done in this book, carries with it an unfortunate potential side effect. It is possible to become so occupied with enemies and dangers that the joys and victories of Christian living do not receive their proper place; yet God would not have it so. Those joys rather energize us and keep us going in the fight itself. God is frequently gracious in giving us some easy victories—especially early in Christian living, as He did with Israel at Jericho—so that we approach our next battle encouraged.

I heard the testimony of a lawyer who asserted that he had received a dramatic demonstration of God's power in his life: His language had changed overnight. He explained, "The day before I was converted, I didn't have enough standard vocabulary left to order ham and eggs in a restaurant. Then literally overnight I found I could not bring myself to use the profanity that had been so common in my speech. I had to learn to talk all over again."

Many Christians can testify of such rapid and radical changes in their own experience. God knows precisely the balance we need. He superintends our steps so that we can walk joyfully with Him. He does not intend that we be morose, negative people who see nothing in life but our problems. And often He encourages us right after a major blunder, as He did with Israel in its famous fight at Gibeon.

The blunder, in fact, created the fight. God had warned Israel against making treaties with the local populations. Israel was to drive out the inhabitants of the land rather than settling for a peaceful co-existence. However, the inhabitants of Gibeon, a major city north of Jerusalem, saw which way the wind was blowing in the Conquest and realized that war against Israel would surely result in their city's annihilation. Rather than moving, they decided to survive by trickery. Secretly abandoning the mutual defense pact they had made with the other cities of the area, they risked everything on their skills of deception.

Disguising themselves as travelers just arriving in Canaan, they appealed to Joshua for a treaty ensuring their safety:

> *From a very far country your servants have come, because of the name of the Lord your God; for we have heard of His fame, and all that He did in Egypt, and all that He did to the two kings of the Amorites. . . . Therefore our elders and all the inhabitants of our country spoke to us, saying, "Take provisions with you for the journey, and go to meet them, and say to them, 'We are your servants; now therefore, make a covenant with us.'"* (Joshua 9:9–11)

Instead of asking counsel of God, Joshua and Israel instituted a cursory investigation and agreed to the Gibeonites' terms, which included a promise to come to their aid should they fall under attack. Later, when Israel discovered that it had been duped by the people of Gibeon, it nevertheless stood by the treaty: "We will let them live, lest wrath be upon us because of the oath which we swore to them . . . but let them be woodcutters and water carriers for all the congregation, as the rulers had promised them" (Joshua 9:20–21).

The Amorite cities of Gibeon's abandoned defense treaty reacted predictably. They attacked Gibeon and laid siege to the town, whereupon the Gibeonites sent a message to Joshua and Israel: "Do not forsake your servants; come up to us quickly, save us and help us, for all the kings of the Amorites who dwell in the mountains have gathered together against us" (Joshua 10:6). Honoring the terms of the ill-advised agreement, Israel left its base camp at Gilgal and moved to relieve the siege of Gibeon. The Amorites were routed, partly due to the direct participation of heaven: "As they fled before Israel and were on the descent of Beth Horon . . . the Lord cast down large hailstones from heaven on them as far as Azekah, and they died. There were more who died from the hailstones than the children of Israel killed with the sword" (Joshua 10:11).

As the afternoon wore on, however, it appeared that many of the Amorites would escape, leading Joshua to pray in an unprecedented way: "Sun, stand still over Gibeon; and Moon, in the Valley of Aijalon" (Joshua 10:12). God answered his prayer, and Israel's victory became complete as a result.

What Really Happened?

The answer to this question is not as obvious as it may seem. If we are driving along in an automobile at fifty miles an hour and suddenly stop, our inertia causes us to fall forward. It seems likely that if the earth ceased its rotation, everybody on the planet would feel the effects. After all, relative to the sun, we are traveling more than a thousand miles an hour right now. We would expect tides to become monstrous should the earth actually stop. With respect to these issues, there have been four basic approaches to answering the question, "What happened at Gibeon?"

Poetical Exaggerations

One approach is to say that Joshua's language is a figure of speech. There are intentional poetical exaggerations in Scripture as in normal human speech, figures of speech we call hyperbole. Israel used one to defend its timidity at Kadesh Barnea: "The cities are great and fortified up to heaven" (Deuteronomy 1:28). The intentional exaggeration causes no confusion in context. When we say, "My feet are killing me," no one expects to read our obituary in the paper the next day.

According to this explanation, Joshua saw that the enemy was about to escape, and he called on God for strength. God answered by refreshing the Israelites, who had marched all night uphill to fight, so that they were able to do a day's fighting in less than half that time. So to them it was as though the day had been lengthened.

I confess that I don't find that explanation satisfying. It doesn't seem to match the qualifications of the text. Nor does it explain the hailstones. If the sun stopping is poetical, what do the hailstones represent? For that reason, most people with a high view of Scripture prefer one of the other three explanations.

A Miracle of Refraction

Some have suggested that a miracle of refraction made it seem as if the sun and moon were out of their places. Several scientists have argued this point astronomically. They say that what happened here was due to a special and rare mirage in the earth's atmosphere that itself could only be attributed to a miracle. The sun kept moving, from Joshua's point of view, but even after going below the horizon there was enough light by which to fight.

That is not an impossible explanation, but I'm not sure that it is completely true to the text, either.

Cooler, Not Longer

Some believe that Joshua did not ask for a longer day but for a cooler one. There is some linguistic evidence to support this. The Hebrew verb *dom*, which many English versions translate "stand still" in Joshua 10:12, usually means "be silent" or "cease." As a result, many students have suggested that Joshua, in the great heat of the day, requested that the sun cease shining, and that God answered by a hailstorm which not only brought cooling clouds to ease the discomfort of the Israelite army, but also destruction to the enemy.

An alternate translation of Joshua 10:12–13: "Be darkened, O sun, in Gibeon, and moon in the valley of Aijalon! And the sun was darkened and the moon turned back."

Retarded Movement

A fourth alternative is to see that the result of the prayer of Joshua was an actual slowing of the sun and moon (or earth). We know, of course, that it is the earth that moves, not the sun. But Joshua's prayer used the language of appearance, which even scientists use. If you check the morning paper, you will find that it refers to "sunset" and "sunrise" in its weather column, although the meteorologists know that the earth does the moving. The language of phenomena forms part of ordinary communication; it isn't a statement of physics. When I fall down, I say, "I fell down." I don't say, "My body moved out of the vertical axis with respect to the center of the earth and was gravitationally attracted to the earth's crust." If we had to use scientifically precise language, we would all starve while trying to get someone to pass the chicken.

Although the orbital mechanics are troublesome for us, it is reasonable to conclude that if God can create the sun and moon, set them in place, and organize their orbits at creation, He can retard their movements without causing harm. He is not a prisoner to His own physical laws, forced to destroy the whole earth in order to give Israel extra time to gain a victory. God is greater than those physical laws He set in motion to govern the universe, and they all work because of Him. To accept a Creator God and then deny Him the ability to govern His creation is illogical, and for that reason I am far more inclined to favor this fourth explanation, even though I can't provide the planetary physics involved. I am content that God could handle the math.

What Difference Does It Make?

I can appreciate the fact that you may be in the fourth level of anesthesia about now. You may be saying, "I can live with any of the four explanations you mentioned. What's so important about coming to a conclusion about what happened at Gibeon thirty-three centuries ago?"

The answer is this. It probably doesn't matter whether you know exactly what happened at the battle of Gibeon. But it does matter how you think about the truthfulness of the God who fought there, because God's truthfulness is the rock upon which faith rests, and self-conquest takes place by faith. How you think about Gibeon is related to how you think about God.

We fight hard because of God's promise
and because of God's power.

Well, you may be thinking, *I can't believe the rotation of the earth slowed down. I've never seen that happen before.* Precisely. That is what the text says too: "There has been no day like that, before it or after it, that the Lord heeded the voice of a man; for the Lord fought for Israel" (Joshua 10:14). Gibeon was a unique event.

DAYS OF VICTORY

In the inner war of self-conquest, God's power may not seem as visually remarkable as the events at Gibeon, but His participation in the war is just as real. We should expect days of great personal victory in our walk with God. God assured Joshua that He was going to give him a great victory (Joshua 10:8). So when he saw the enemy escaping, he had a good reason to ask God to do something that had never been done before. *The person who gets to see God do great things is the one who is in the midst of fighting for His interests.* Refusing to engage in inner spiritual change cheats us of many a privilege.

Honoring Commitments

Gibeon also teaches that integrity means honoring commitments that, in the wisdom of hindsight, we later regret making. Can you imagine how tempting it would have been for Joshua to do nothing when the Gibeonites pleaded for his help? He might have rationalized that he should simply let the Amorites rid Israel of a problem. Joshua, however, refused to do so; he knew that once you have made a commitment in God's name, you stay with it.

May I suggest a rather obvious application? People sometimes enter into marriages that never should have been made. After a while, it seems the expedient thing to do is to take the easy way out, even when we lack biblical authority; but that isn't God's way. Christian warriors stand by their covenants, because their integrity means more to them than their comforts.

Miracles with Effort

Expecting God to do great things for us makes personal effort more, not less important. Joshua expected God to give him the victory, so what did he do? Did he get a good night's sleep, review the troops, have a nice breakfast, and then start for Gibeon?

Hardly. He led Israel in a forced march, uphill, all night long, for thirty miles and attacked at dawn (Joshua 10:9). Once the battle was joined, he and the army attacked all day long. He refused to withdraw because of fatigue or from lack of will. He fought hard because he knew God had promised victory. That is the way the holy war against sin in our lives has to be fought. Give any quarter, any rest to it, and you lose. We fight hard because of God's promise and because of God's power. Our progress in self-conquest comes in direct proportion to the confidence we have in God's greatness.

One of the giants of biblical scholarship a couple of generations ago was a man by the name of Robert Dick Wilson. Wilson taught at Princeton Seminary in the days when the school still maintained a high view of Scripture. One of Wilson's students was a young man by the name of Donald Grey Barnhouse who, several years after graduating, was invited back to preach in seminary chapel. When Barnhouse arrived, he noticed that Wilson had taken a place near the front to hear him. When the service was over, his old Hebrew professor came up to Barnhouse and said, "I am glad I came to hear you today, and I am especially glad that you are a 'big-godder.' When my boys come back, I always come to see if they are 'big-godders' or 'little-godders,' and then I know what their ministry will be like."

Barnhouse asked him to explain what he meant. He said, "Well, some men have a little god, and they are always in trouble with him. He can't do any miracles. He can't take care of the inspiration of the Scriptures and their preservation and transmission to us. They have a little god, and I call them 'little-godders.' Then there are those who have a great God. He speaks, and it is done. He commands, and it stands fast. He knows how to show himself strong on behalf of those who fear Him. You have a great God, and He will bless your ministry" —a prophecy that, happily, was borne out by history.

The true greatness of our God is that He has come down to us. If you are a Christian believer, then you have experienced the greatest miracle God has ever performed: to overcome the prejudice of a heart in flight away from God and win the affection of a rebel. God's signature in creation and all the other miracles of all time are merely preparatory steps taken by God in order to achieve this greatest of wonders. When a Christian turns away from his old man and puts to death the deeds of his body, he engages in a battle he cannot lose as long as he continues to fight.

CHAPTER ELEVEN

PRISONERS
OF WAR

What I am doing, I do not understand.
—THE APOSTLE PAUL (ROMANS 7:15)

Most people who have made sincere efforts to eradicate their faults have at some point become discouraged by their inability to subjugate their own inner person. Sometimes we make the job harder by tolerating a measure of interest in a sinful practice that in time causes us to stumble. The problem is illustrated in the experience of a British officer who was serving as part of that country's Indian army back in the twenties. One of his servants called his attention to a Bengal tiger cub that had been abandoned by its mother and that in the natural course of things would have died. He adopted it as a pet and provided its food and supervision, and it grew up in his house as a member of his family.

Bengal tigers cannot deny their nature, however. One day in what would have been considered its young adulthood, the animal was lying on the floor next to the officer's rocking chair. It was a hot afternoon; the officer had just returned from a strenuous expedition, and he fell asleep in the chair. The tiger began to lick the officer's hand as it dangled in his sleeping position. During the day's exertions, he had received a cut on that hand. As the animal licked it, the wound began to bleed. The tiger tasted his owner's blood for the first time, and his licking took on new interest. The officer awakened in time to see his family pet snarling in a most unfriendly manner, ready to have him for dinner. What he had allowed room for in his life, thinking it posed no threat, turned out to create mortal danger for him.

That's how sin behaves. Things that seem innocent and even friendly we suddenly discover to be deadly. What we think we can take or leave can become addictive. Issues that we thought were far behind us as part of our non-Christian experience can rise up and destroy us.

God has called every Christian believer to adopt a militant attitude toward himself. We come into the Christian life in varying stages of character development. Some have the advantages of growing up in a home where both parents are godly, helping them get a head start on self-conquest; but even those without such advantages figure out early that there is a huge distance between where they are and where God wants them to be spiritually.

That is a situation that is anticipated by the Scriptures. God tells us at the outset of our Christian lives two facts that serve as the boundaries of Christian living. Fact number one: We can be different; we can be conformed to the image of Christ over time. Fact number two: We cannot be different without His help. So we are supposed to be developing people on the one hand; and on the other hand we must be dependent people. God has placed us between these two poles. On our worst day we are important to God and filled with possibilities. On our best day we are far less than we ought to be. So we avoid despair on one end and self-deception on the other.

WHOM WE WILL SERVE

For better or worse, the option of absolute independence is not open to creatures. We cannot choose total autonomy; we can only decide who will be in charge of our lives. Sometimes that choice is made without adequate thought, as in this true account by a victim of the slave trade:

Strangers with pale faces passed by our village one day and dropped a small piece of red flannel on the path that ran down to the river. At first everyone was afraid, but finally someone went out and picked it up. It was the most beautiful thing we had ever seen. In Africa we had very few pretty things, and we had no red cloth. . . . Then we saw another piece of red flannel a little farther down the path. We all ran to get it.

Then another piece was spotted. . . . All along the path were pieces of the red flannel. We all began running along the path picking up the pieces of the red cloth and laughing. We ran all the way to the river. We stood there by the river looking at the pieces of cloth, marveling at the pale men who were so stupid to lose such beautiful cloth. Then someone yelled, "Look!"

There on the far side of the river we could see another piece of the cloth. Almost everyone jumped in and swam to the other side. Only old people and babies stayed behind.

The best swimmer grabbed the first piece, but we could see that there were more pieces along the path. We ran and walked for a long time that day picking up the pieces and laughing. As we reached the top of the last hill before the ocean, we saw a ship. We had never seen such a large boat. We followed the trail of cloth up a plank onto the ship and finally we even went down inside the ship. Then the gate was chained and we could not climb out. I guess the slower runners stood on the shore and watched the pale men sail the ship away with us, their family members and friends, on board. I never saw my village again.[1]

The low point of Israel's experience at Kadesh Barnea came when the people decided to return to slavery. Centuries later, as the Levites confessed the sins of the nation, the memory was still a bitter one: "They refused to obey, and they were not mindful of Your wonders that You did among them. But they hardened their necks, and in their rebellion they appointed a leader to return to their bondage" (Nehemiah 9:17).

Rebellion always leads to slavery, whether in Israel or in the Christian who decides that "just this once" he will indulge himself and violate the clear instruction of God's Word. Later, he may come to realize that what began as a whim now has a grip on his will. Slavery being an unpalatable word these days, modern man prefers to call the problem a bad habit or addictive behavior, but slavery it is.

A Culture of Slavery

Those of us who want to conquer enslaving habits find little help in the culture. After a century of being indoctrinated by Dr. Sigmund Freud, our world has nearly lost altogether the biblical concept of responsibility. Today, we regard enslaved people either as ill or as victims. And according to our culture, once a person's illness or antagonist is identified, he is therefore excused from responsibility entirely until he is "cured." The process long ago passed being ridiculous, to wit:

- Several years ago in Oregon, a credit union manager was charged with eighty-three counts of embezzlement. Prosecutors computed that she had stolen $630,000 over a period of six years. The defendant told a Eugene jury that her hands may have taken the money but that her heart, mind, and spirit were innocent, because some other personality within her did it.
- In California, a young man and his parents filed a lawsuit against the county where he lived, asking for at least $700,000 in compensation. They were seeking redress for the teen's total disability, the result of an auto accident. Their petition explained that he and some of his friends had decided to celebrate and had in the process become much the worse for drink. The young co-plaintiff, sitting in the backseat of the car, had stuck his head out the window to lose his cookies just as the driver careened off the road. The resulting crash jammed the victim's head into a tree, resulting in paralysis. The lawsuit claimed that it was the county's fault that the tree was so close to the road.
- A Wisconsin appeals court recently upheld a lower court's ruling that a golf course in Wausau owed one of its members a substantial amount of money. The trial court declared that the club was 51 percent responsible for the golfer's needing nine root canals and twenty-three dental crowns. It seems that he had tripped on his golf spikes and fallen on his face on the brick path outside the clubhouse. The plaintiff's attorneys successfully contended that he would not have fallen had the path been instead a smooth concrete sidewalk. The trial court determined that only 49 percent of the accident was due to the plaintiff's having con-

sumed thirteen drinks that evening, leaving him with a blood-alcohol level of .28 ninety minutes after the fall. (For those who don't follow such statistics, a blood-alcohol level of .28 means that you are about three times more impaired than needed to merit arrest for DUI.)

It is an article of faith in the Western world today that freedom comes from fleeing responsibility. If we can find someone on whom to blame our troubles, we can feel better about ourselves. If we can get an authoritative person to label us a victim, that's even better, and there may be money in it for us.

> *The Spirit of God leads us into freedom, not into slavery.*

I doubt that I need to pound the pulpit too hard to convince you that this notion will not hold up in scriptural court. The Bible teaches that at the last judgment God will bring before Himself the dead, both exalted and lowly, and judge them according to their deeds. People will reap forever what they have sown. In the end, every person will have to face the consequences of his own choices. There will be no place to hide at that great tribunal. God will be treating people as responsible whether the culture labels them responsible or not.

He likewise holds us accountable in this life, albeit with less severe consequences, for our daily choices. A penalty He sometimes chooses to impose in this life is enslavement to our sins. The Bible contains a considerable body of teaching on what we call today addictive behavior. For example, the apostle Paul wrote, "You did not receive the spirit of bondage [leading] again to fear" (Romans 8:15). The Spirit of God leads us into freedom, not into slavery. If we choose bondage, we have left the path of the Spirit—yet God, as much as He encourages it, does not compel us to walk with Him.

Christians in Slavery

God can cause Christians, if we are sufficiently willful, to become enslaved to our own choices: "If you live according to the flesh, you will die; but if by the Spirit you put to death the deeds of the body, you will live" (Romans 8:13). It is clear from this verse that Christians have two lifestyles they can follow. Although the carnal mind has no choice but to live according to the flesh, believers have a choice. We can live according to the flesh, which typically involves flight from responsibility, or we can by the Spirit put to death such a lifestyle. When a Christian goes his own way and lives according to the flesh, he isn't really living; he is decaying. Paul described this when he wrote about wayward Christian women in 1 Timothy 5:6. He said, "She who lives in pleasure is dead while she lives."

Christians can be severely judgmental of other Christians who make these foolish choices. One of the ways we often do so is in asserting that such people don't belong to Christ at all. We reason that people who are enslaved to sins to which we are not enslaved couldn't be Christians. People who haven't been captured themselves often seem eager to condemn those who are caught up in drink, in promiscuity, or in homosexuality. But before we take out the carving knives, we need at least to understand this phenomenon biblically. If we do, we may wield a more compassionate blade.

Paul was addressing enslavement when he wrote: "Brethren, if a man is overtaken in any trespass, you who are spiritual restore such a one in a spirit of gentleness, considering yourself lest you also be tempted" (Galatians 6:1). Clearly, a Christian is in view here. Spiritual people cannot *restore* someone to a place he or she has never been. Paul's counsel concerns bringing a believer back into an effective relationship with the local church and with the Lord.

The Greek word he uses to describe the wayward Christian is *prolambano,* which literally means "to overtake." The word picture suggests a person who has become enmeshed in wrong behavior (a trespass, to use Paul's term) and who is running away from the consequences of it. However, the person can't run fast enough, and his trespass has now caught up with him. He has become tangled in the results of his behavior.

In fact, he has been captured to the degree that he cannot rescue himself, so the apostle directs the mature leadership of the church to go to him and restore him. They are to accomplish three goals: (1) They are to approach him in a spirit of gentleness with a view toward his restoration; (2) they are to tell him to stop it; and (3) they are to scrutinize their own hearts to make sure they are not drawn into the attractions of the sin in which the wayward member finds himself.

It is worth noting that even mature Christians need to be on the alert, guarding their minds when confronted with addictive behavior. They also need to curb any tendency to harshness. Gentleness is the way to approach someone who has been captured and enslaved to sin. Would that Christians had always been noted for their gentleness and concern for other believers who find themselves in the grips of sinful enslavements! Often we behave in ways that are anything but therapeutic.

THE POWER OF ENSLAVING SINS

Paul includes in his letters several lists of sins that can be enslaving. For example, he wrote, "I have written to you not to keep company with anyone named a brother, who is sexually immoral, or covetous, or an idolater, or a reviler, or a drunkard, or an extortioner—not even to eat with such a person" (1 Corinthians 5:11). Such are the kinds of trespasses that draw people into their clutches. Their public nature, Paul explains here, requires the church at large to forego even the normal kinds of fellowship with people who persist in them.

A word of clarification may be helpful here. Galatians 6:1 instructs mature Christians to restore people who are enslaved. First Corinthians 5:11 warns even against eating with people who are enslaved. One approach is gentle, the other severe. How are these two approaches to be reconciled?

The preferred strategy depends on the timing. Galatians 6:1 recognizes that anyone can be captured for a time by an addictive behavior. Every sin is sinful, but there are certain categories of sins that have a premium attached to them because they enslave the people who engage in them. Alcoholism is an obvious example. If you have ever had a problem with drink in your life, you know just how powerful the pull of addictive drinking can be. Promiscuity is the same way: It's habit-forming. So is materialism—what Paul calls covetousness in 1 Corinthians 5:11. It is possible for people to be captured almost before they know it. What should the church do in a case like that? The answer is "Invoke Galatians 6:1." Send mature church leaders to the guilty and gently rebuke them with an eye to restoring them to fellowship with God.

But what if that doesn't work? I have been involved in a number of situations similar to what Paul describes in Galatians 6:1, when I have gone with church leaders in just that spirit of gentleness to attempt to restore a wayward brother. Sometimes it goes well and the person does repent. Much of the time, it does not. Enslavement, after all, is enslavement.

So what do you do if the person steadfastly (or even arrogantly) tells you that his spiritual condition is none of your business? What do you do if the person refuses to, in the words of the Lord Jesus, "pay attention to the church" (see Matthew 18:17)? You apply 1 Corinthians 5:11. The last line of defense for a church is to separate itself from people who refuse to call their enslavement by its real name. If a person says, "I'm enslaved, but I want to change," you help him. If he says, "I'm OK, and I don't need your meddling," you have to separate yourself from him. Even then, you don't treat him as an enemy, Paul says, but as a wayward brother (2 Thessalonians 3:15). Galatians 6 comes first, then 1 Corinthians 5.

Please note that all this describes therapeutic behavior toward a Christian. There is no warrant whatever for separating yourself from non-Christians who engage in these things. If you feel at risk, you can separate yourself in the interests of not being drawn into those sins, but you cannot separate yourself because God insists that you do (1 Corinthians 5:10), or (even worse) because you feel a moral superiority over the enslaved person. We are to be more cautious in our relationships with Christians than with those outside the faith. With the former, it helps to know how to help trapped people.

Thinking Clearly About Slavery

Thinking clearly about enslavement means distinguishing the irresponsibility by which a person is first captured and the power by which he continues to be enslaved. In one sense, adulterers are victims—but only after their first choice to commit adultery. After being in the net for a while, its attractions seem preferable to the freedom outside. One of sin's worst penalties is to make us irrational.

In other words, we can't help people by simply criticizing them. Yes, of course, they shouldn't have dabbled in transgressions that were clearly so powerful. Yes, they were foolish in even dancing around the edges of a fire that could burn them.

But the question that we eventually face is, "What can I do to help?" One thing that won't help is condemnation. A different approach is needed. For a Christian to overcome drink or homosexuality or a pattern of cheating or deception is nearly as great a victory as conversion. It is a testimony to the power of Christ that He can rescue a person in the grip of an awful master.

God made us to serve; we are going to have a master of one sort or another: "Do you not know that to whom you present yourselves slaves to obey, you are that one's slaves whom you obey, whether of sin leading to death, or of obedience leading to righteousness?" (Romans 6:16). The very idea of being a slave repels us, but if Scripture can be trusted, we are all slaves because we are creatures. The moment I present myself to a sin to indulge in it, I am its slave. If I do it often enough, I may look around one day and find that my chains are too powerful to break. Paul says that that is conduct unbecoming a Christian believer, and ultimately self-destructive.

Where Slavery Begins

Enslavement starts with the first drink, the first sexual escapade, the first theft, the first choice to cheat. If Scripture teaches anything, it is that no one is exempt from the possibility of spiritual enslavement. We kid ourselves if we think we have passed the point in our spiritual development where becoming addicted to something is beyond us. It always starts with the first choice.

Will picking up a copy of *Playboy* or clicking on a pornographic Website destroy your life? Not by itself, but it is a first step that could easily lead there. Will cheating on your income tax turn you into a materialist? Not necessarily, but then again you can't guarantee that you will stop cheating once you have started.

Where Slavery Leads

Where enslavement commonly leads is to self-condemnation and shame. We do something often enough that we know is wrong and we spend an undue amount of time whipping ourselves for our weakness. And that is the problem. We *are* weak in the face of addictive sins. We need all the strength we can get and a lot of strength we don't have.

Most of the time we have to have help. That is why God says to find the most spiritually mature people available and send them to restore a brother caught in a trespass. He is unlikely to be able to tear himself loose at that point, and he needs the best help he can get.

If you're in the grip of something, don't bemoan your fate or whip yourself for your weakness. Find somebody you can trust to help you. It won't be easy, even with help; but it at least becomes possible.

Where Slavery Ends

Enslavement can end in a broken lifestyle or even in death. A powerful verse in Proverbs gives a dramatic picture of the principle: "The mouth of an immoral woman is a deep pit; he who is abhorred by the Lord will fall there" (Proverbs 22:14). Notice how cause and effect are portrayed in the verse. Christians often see a person involved in promiscuity or adultery and wonder, *This person is a Christian, and he is getting away with a sinful lifestyle. Why doesn't God do something?*

Proverbs 22:14 notes that, at least in many cases, the reason that person is in a sinful lifestyle is that God has already done something. He has sentenced the offender to serve time in chains. The "victim" is described in a shocking way: "He who is abhorred by the Lord." How does that happen? Doesn't God love everybody? How is it that He comes to abhor someone? Is this some sort of irrational and arbitrary hatred on His part?

Of course not. Another proverb gives the answer: "He who is often rebuked, and hardens his neck, will suddenly be destroyed, and that without remedy" (Proverbs 29:1). What is assumed in Proverbs 22:14 is this process of being "often rebuked." The person whom the Lord abhors is the one who will not turn around even though he is often warned. He "hardens his neck"—he becomes stubborn—and then one day he discovers himself in the clutches of a power that destroys his marriage and even his life. He is broken suddenly; he is broken in a way that can't be fixed, but his peril comes at the end of a long series of unheeded corrections.

HOW TO DEFEAT ENSLAVING SINS

There is only one surefire way to stay out of enslaving sins, and that is never to start down the road of enslavement. If you know that sexual sin is typically enslaving, and you know that lust is provoked in the realm of thoughts first, then stay away from things that provoke lust in the realm of thoughts. If you tend to overspend, don't spend your spare time flipping through catalogs. If you are drawn to shady deals, don't sit down and think through new ways to make a fast buck or even listen to someone else's ideas on the subject.

God wants us to be creatures of habit— but those habits are to be habits of holiness.

I'm afraid that many Christians spend their whole Christian lives in the grip of some enslaving sin because they are too embarrassed to go and ask someone for help. That is a shame, because there are ways out of the cages we inhabit, usually involving a measure of accountability to someone. Although that might be a little uncomfortable, it is far easier (and far wiser) than spending your life ashamed of yourself for being in the grip of a dominant habit.

On the other hand, if you want to help other people avoid a life of slavery, you have two possibilities. One is preventative, the other corrective. When you see someone who is about to be captured by a trespass, warning him off before the hooks are set too deeply is the best way to be of help.

If you miss that opportunity, then often the only remedy is prayer combined with gentle correction. Paul wrote Timothy,

A servant of the Lord must not quarrel but be gentle to all, able to teach, patient, in humility correcting those who are in opposition, if God perhaps will grant them repentance, so that they may know the truth, and that they may come to their senses and escape the snare of the devil, having been taken captive by him to do his will. (2 Timothy 2:24–26)

God may or may not grant him repentance. God may or may not allow him to come to his senses and break free of a life of captivity. There are no guarantees of liberty when sound counsel is spurned often enough.

God wants us to be creatures of habit—but those habits are to be habits of holiness. We can develop patterns of righteousness just as we develop patterns of unrighteousness. In other words, we need to choose our Master and present ourselves anew to Him each day. Good habits, as well as bad ones, are strengthened by repetition.

RETREAT

Most of us would live by faith
if we knew the rewards would be
forthcoming within two weeks.[1]
—VANCE HAVNER

The question I have received most often over my three decades of ministry is this: "Why does it take me so long to get better?" Or, to put it another way, "Why is progress in the Christian life so difficult?" The commonness of that question provides a hint about why so many people don't make long-term progress in Christian growth. The warfare we are in is long and hard, and one weapon is missing from the arsenals of many a believer: persistence. Lots of Christians give up their inner warfare from the sheer length of the struggle. No matter how many times they put the deeds of the body to death, the sins rise from the grave and come at them again. It is enough to discourage a person.

The people of Israel understood. Their failure to persevere led to one of the most remarkable episodes in human history. God Himself stepped out of heaven and came to earth to deliver the bad news about their spiritual retreat. Here is how the event is described: "The Angel of the Lord came up from Gilgal to Bochim, and said: 'I led you up from Egypt and brought you to the land of which I swore to your fathers; and I said, "I will never break My covenant with you. And you shall make no covenant with the inhabitants of this land; you shall tear down their altars." But you have not obeyed My voice'" (Judges 2:1–2). In exchange for His wholehearted commitment to them, they had broken the covenant.

The name of the place was Bochim—meaning, literally, "Weepers." The place received its name from this event. God was pronouncing judgment against a whole generation of people who came into the land with great potential, yet lost the war.

You may be saying to yourself, "How can you say, 'They lost the war,' when they came into possession of the land? Didn't they take over? Didn't they win the Land of Promise?"

The answer is, "Yes and no": "yes" in that they now owned a homeland; "no" in the sense that it wasn't the whole land. The proof appears in Judges 2:2–3, where the Angel of the Lord asserts, "You have not obeyed My voice. . . . Therefore I also said, 'I will not drive them out before you; but they shall be thorns in your side.'" Israel did not get the job done.

THE WEAPON LEFT BEHIND

The nation of Israel failed because it lacked persistence. Persistence is one of the greatest of the virtues described in the New Testament. I like a little poem that summarizes how important it is:

> *Don't worry if your job is small*
> *And your rewards are few,*
> *Remember that the mighty oak*
> *Was once a nut like you!*

Like the oak, we need to persist. The Israelites did not persist. They fought with the Canaanites, to be sure. They drove many of them out of the land. But some of them proved to be tough opponents. A summary of Israel's behavior appears in Judges 1:28: "When Israel was strong, they put the Canaanites under tribute, but did not completely drive them out." In other words, the Israelites made their enemies pay taxes, and then settled down to a comfortable accommodation of their enemies. They did not keep fighting. They gave up before the battle was over.

The book of Judges relates a list of specific failures in the verses that follow. The Ephraimites compromised with the inhabitants of Gezer: "Nor did Ephraim drive out the Canaanites who dwelt in Gezer; so the Canaanites dwelt in Gezer among them" (Judges 1:29). The Zebulonites failed to take a couple of major cities (see Judges 1:30). The Asherites did the same, as did the people of Naphtali (Judges 1:31–33).

The Danites did next to nothing: "The Amorites forced the children of Dan into the mountains, for they would not allow them to come down to the valley" (Judges 1:34). The tribe of Dan eventually moved a hundred miles away. Even when Ephraim and Manasseh became more powerful, they tried to expel the coastal inhabitants and couldn't do it, either (see Judges 1:35). They taxed the Amorites and let them live where they wanted. We still see David going into battle against the Philistines four hundred years after Israel entered the land. His wars were made necessary by the refusal of the tribe of Dan to drive the Philistines off its assigned portion.

THE COST OF DISOBEDIENCE

And what price did the nation have to pay for this disobedience? "Therefore I also said, 'I will not drive them out before you; but they shall be thorns in your side, and their gods shall be a snare to you'" (Judges 2:3). Thorns are generally not lethal, but they are bothersome. From the time of Bochim on, the people who were left became a pain in the side of Israel. The Israelites never could get away from them. The pagans kept God's people from enjoying what ought to have been theirs. Most important, God determined that He would not drive Israel's enemies out. They had given up on their enemies, and He had (in a sense) given up on them; hence, their great sorrow. They understood the gravity of this terrible announcement.

The events of Bochim are repeated many times over in individual Christian lives. Any time we throw in the towel and try to reach an accommodation with a sin in our lives, it becomes a thorn in our side, a constant irritant and a reminder that we have work yet to do.

Israel also paid another price: "Their gods shall be a snare to you" (Judges 2:3). The people's attraction to the gods of their enemies caused them to regress spiritually. They did not simply settle in the land and keep a separate existence from their enemies. The religion of Canaan appealed to Israel's baser instincts. Their devotion to the Lord was always on the edge of erosion because of the fleshly temptations at the local pagan temple. Snares are deceptive influences that you don't see until it's too late.

Sin is like that. It sneaks up on you when you least expect it. God never wants Christians to relax when it comes to the spiritual battle. To fight effectively, we must understand the nature of the enemy, the sin that lives inside us waiting for expression. Gaining such an understanding is more complex than it seems. In one way, all sins are alike. In another way, however, they differ greatly.

THE COMMONALITIES OF SINS

All sins separate people from God. It takes just one to make a person imperfect. God, by contrast, accepts no imperfections. He can have no fellowship with anyone who does not share His holiness. James says, "For whoever shall keep the whole law, and yet stumble in one point, he is guilty of all. For He who said, 'Do not commit adultery,' also said, 'Do not murder.' Now if you do not commit adultery, but you do murder, you have become a transgressor of the law" (2:10–11).

In that sense, all sins are alike. It doesn't matter whether you murder someone or merely envy him some privilege, you become a transgressor of God's law either way.

All sins also require a death to atone for them. The central teaching of the Bible is that sins can be forgiven if a person depends on Jesus Christ to pay for them. As a perfect Person, He was qualified to lay down a perfect life for imperfect people. So long as any person is willing to accept what Jesus did for him, he can be forgiven and have eternal life.

But there is another sense in which that is also true. I have to die to myself over and over again in dealing with sins on a daily basis. One part of me desperately wants to yield control of myself to the pleasures that sin offers. I have to put my old man to death day after day in order to deal with the sins I face as a Christian.

David Martyn Lloyd-Jones was a surgeon, a very successful one, who decided that he would rather operate on souls than on bodies and thus left medicine for pastoral ministry. He was chosen by G. Campbell Morgan as his successor at Westminster Tabernacle in London, and for many years he sustained a rich ministry both in the pulpit and in his writing. People admired him as much for his praying as for his preaching. He exuded a godly demeanor that was always fresh and appealing.

*Some sins tend to disillusion
other people about the truth of the gospel.*

At the peak of his effectiveness in ministry he wrote a paragraph that describes the difference between the way people in the church viewed him and how he viewed himself:

> They see only that which is good in me; they see me only at my best. I shudder when I realize how unworthy I am and how ignorant they are of the dark and hidden recesses of my soul where all that is devilish and hideous reigns supreme, at times breaking through onto the surface and causing a turmoil that God and I alone know of.[2]

I would be hard pressed to name someone who exhibited a more consistent character and a more godly example than Martyn Lloyd-Jones. Yet I think any honest preacher would agree with the good doctor's assessment. None of us feels worthy of the work we do, because we know that there is a huge distance between what God wants us to be and what we are. Dr. Jones's comments, of course, apply whether you are in the ministry or not. The good news is, the more we see our flaws and recognize the work we have to do, the more likely it is that we are living the way we should.

Sins separate us from God. If they don't do it eternally, because we are Christians, they still keep us from enjoying Him and they ruin our fellowship. They also require a death to deal with them. In these two senses, sins are alike.

THE DIFFERENCES BETWEEN SINS

However, sins are unlike each other when it comes, for example, to their social consequences. Some produce pain and discomfort only for the one who commits them. Others lay waste to people who are near enough to be caught in the backwash. Almost all addictions fit into this latter category. The man who compulsively gambles doesn't merely lose money, but he also mortgages the future of the people he professes to love and destroys his ability to advance God's work. The person who is addicted to alcohol commonly abuses family members either verbally or physically or both, to say nothing of the financial destruction that is frequently involved or the shame of having to watch somebody you love destroy himself. The person who is addicted to sexual pleasures, even the ones that don't involve immorality with another person, corrupts his ability to deal openly and in a healthy way with a mate and with other people.

Sins also differ in their religious effects. Some sins tend to disillusion other people about the truth of the gospel. My son, Tim, once worked in a restaurant alongside a young man who had become rather embittered against spiritual things because of the behavior of some of the churchgoers he had met. "Jeremy" had once worked in an establishment across the street from a church whose parishioners often took Sunday lunch there. Certain worshipers routinely asked for Bloody Marys with their meals, but specified that the drinks were to be served in coffee cups so that other churchgoers in the restaurant would be unaware that they were drinking. Understandably, Jeremy had developed a strong case of resistance to the gospel.

Then there are sins that take so much of a person's mental and emotional energy that he has little left to pursue spiritual interests. He is robbed of the ability and the inclination to serve God by the extent and the way he serves himself.

Sins likewise differ in their personal consequences. Embezzlement may end a promising career in banking or securities for someone at the same time it produces a jail term. Even when it happens before conversion, a sin committed in the public eye will tend to discredit anyone who might ever aspire to leadership in the ministry of the church.

Sins also differ in their ability to dominate lives. Certain practices can gain such a grip over us that we feel powerless to overcome them. Sin is by its very nature addictive, and certain sins can become life-dominating. Sexual sins are particularly destructive in this way, because they are virtually always done in secret. As a result, they generally require that a person become a skilled liar and a hypocrite in order to cover them up.

Sins differ considerably, and perhaps most markedly, in their ability to discourage us. It is this aspect of sin that is particularly germane to the experience of Bochim. Israel fought the Canaanites for thirty years. That's a long time to fight. When you've been going up against the same people for thirty years, you begin to wonder if victory is possible. You wonder if it is a good idea to risk your life every day for a victory that you are not sure can be won. After thirty years you learn to rationalize like a bandit: "Why not just permit the Canaanites to live in the land? Why not try peaceful coexistence? After all, isn't it true that God said we shouldn't kill? Let's just let them live here among us and try to show them that there is a better way to live. Let's show them the superiority of the worship of Yahweh. Let's transform them instead of them transforming us." Right.

Certain types of sins are especially powerful in their ability to discourage us. I'm thinking now of what we often call bad habits, those acts of disobedience that just don't seem to go away. We keep fighting the same battles we have fought for years. Somewhere along the way, it is tempting to settle for less and say, "Let's try to contain them instead of eliminating them."

That's why God went to such lengths to tell the people of Israel that the worst mistake they could make was to yield to thinking like that. They had to persist. They had to keep fighting because the alternative was unthinkable. Once you accommodate a sin in your life, that sin becomes the equivalent of what the Canaanites were in the Holy Land.

The Canaanites proved to be world-class persuaders for their religion. They managed to make untold thousands of Israelites—people who had seen God perform miracle after miracle—throw over their faith and bow down and worship Canaanite idols. The Canaanites, losers in the physical war, nevertheless were the winners in the ideological and spiritual struggle for the hearts of people who lived in the land.

That's why the last and in many ways most important weapon in the Christian's arsenal is persistence. If we use courage, faith, and all the rest, we still have to keep using them even when we don't see the results we want. The stakes are too high to give up, though we don't always realize it.

On a commuter flight from Portland, Maine, to Boston, pilot Henry Dempsey heard an unusual noise near the rear of the small aircraft. He turned the controls over to his co-pilot and went back to check things out. As he reached the tail section, the plane hit an air pocket, and Dempsey was tossed against the rear door. He instantly discovered the source of the mysterious noise. The rear door had not been properly latched prior to takeoff, and it flew open. He was instantly sucked out of the jet.

The co-pilot, seeing the red light that indicated an open door, radioed the nearest airport, requesting permission to make an emergency landing. He reported that the pilot had fallen out of the plane, and he requested a helicopter search of that area of the ocean.

After the plane landed, emergency personnel found Henry Dempsey holding on to the outdoor ladder of the aircraft that was built into the rear door. Somehow he had caught the ladder, held on for ten minutes as the plane flew 200 M.P.H. at an altitude of four thousand feet, and then, at landing, kept his head from hitting the runway, just a few inches away. It took airport personnel several minutes to pry Dempsey's fingers from the ladder. When you know the stakes, you tend to persevere.

It is possible to develop a biblical attitude about the spiritual battles we are in, the kind of mental toughness that refuses to accept a loss. In my younger days, I played basketball at UCLA under legendary coach John Wooden. We won the NCAA title twice during my college years, and one of the reasons was Coach Wooden's use of a zone press. The standard defensive tactic at the time called for a casual retreat to the defensive end of the floor after scoring a basket. The zone press was a radical departure from that approach. Whenever we scored, we began to play an aggressive style of defense immediately. We conceded nothing, not even allowing our opponents to make an uncontested inbounds pass. We harassed our opponents and pressured them into losing their composure.

The tactics worked exceptionally well. Usually at some point during the first half, the other team would come unravelled. A bad pass would lead to an easy basket—and more defensive pressure, and more easy baskets. Often we scored ten or twenty points in a row. The best teams in America struggled against the zone press. Our hard work always wore them down at some point.

One team, however, tore our press to shreds. No matter how hard we tried, we never seemed to contain them consistently. They never became rattled, rarely threw the ball away, and made it into the frontcourt with a minimum of difficulty. Who were these wizards who accomplished what the best teams in America could not? Our second string. They made a habit of embarrassing us every day in practice.

> *If we win the battle today, but all our confidence is in ourselves, then we haven't really won much.*

Several things accounted for their success. They were good athletes. They understood the theory behind the press. They knew what to expect, and they didn't have ten thousand fans screaming at them.

However, one reason they did so well was their mental toughness. They decided that since they were going to be facing this annoying defense every day, they might as well learn how to cope with it. It wasn't going to go away. Their future hopes for playing time were connected with how well they practiced, so they kept cool and learned to cope with the pressure.

That's exactly the quality that the Bible calls endurance. The Greek word for endurance combines two terms that together mean "staying under." The word picture suggested is "staying put under pressure." That's exactly what we need when doing battle with a sin that we have fought before. We need staying power—the quality that maintains its poise and learns to cope.

"The testing of your faith produces endurance," explains James. "And let endurance have its perfect result, so that you may be perfect and complete, lacking in nothing" (James 1:3–4 NASB). James's words suggest that we will find it easier to give up than to develop the quality of endurance. That is particularly true when we have been praying and asking for God's help and it does not seem to be forthcoming. We can easily conclude that God cares little about whether we defeat our sins.

However, God puts us between two psychological boundaries when we become Christians. On the one hand, we can be different. On the other hand, we cannot be different without His help. Which of these two boundaries do you think we have more trouble with? Certainly it is the second; and that is where the role of prayer assumes its proper place. When we are trying to grow and do battle with the old man, we find our toughest test in the realm of dependence. We pray and ask God's help in overcoming sin in our lives, and often when the crunch comes we fail. That dismays us, because it seems to us that God certainly ought to help us do what He asks of us.

He is even more interested, however, in our learning dependence. If we win the battle today, but all our confidence is in ourselves, then we haven't really won much. The battle resumes each day, and each resumption brings the necessity of renewing our conscious attachment to our Commander in Chief, who provides us with strength to persist.

Our staying power has to be built on biblical realities, and one of those realities is that our fight is a continuing one. If we lose a battle today, we haven't lost as long as we keep fighting. It is only when we give in that we have really lost.

Israel's lack of persistence could have been prevented if the people had recalled the charge Moses issued before going into battle. In the plains of Moab, he called on the people of Israel to take his words with them: "Now this is the commandment, and these are the statutes and judgments which the Lord your God has commanded to teach you, that you may observe them in the land which you are crossing over to possess" (Deuteronomy 6:1). The same charge applies to people who are going into battle with themselves.

THE GOALS OF THE CHARGE

Moses' purpose (and the Lord's) in providing the charge was three-fold: to promote obedience, godly fear, and blessing.

Obeying the Lord

Moses gave God's statutes and judgments not for their curiosity, but for their conformity: "that you may observe them" (Deuteronomy 6:1). It is intriguing how in some circles conformity is regarded as the worst of all social problems. People are not supposed to be alike in any way. Individuality is crucial to personal success. If anybody else has rules, we are supposed to be at pains to avoid giving them any credence.

But conformity to biblical morals is not a crime; it is not a sign of weakness, or stupidity. Morality is not the invention of man, but the gift of God to give humanity a fighting chance to genuinely enjoy life.

Fearing the Lord

Moses' charge was designed as "that you may observe them in the land which you are crossing over to possess, that you may fear the Lord your God" (Deuteronomy 6:1–2). Please notice the relationship of obedience to godly fear. One produces the other, and, surprisingly perhaps, obedience is the one mentioned first. You tend to respect people you make a habit of obeying, and that was what Moses was after. He wanted the Israelites to have a healthy respect for the true and the living God.

That is what fearing the Lord is all about. There is a kind of fear that avoids what is feared; but that is not the kind of fear that Scripture commends. The fear that avoids is based not on obedience, but on disobedience, and it comes from offending the person who is feared. What Moses was advocating is the kind of fear that avoids offense. The person who fears God in this way would rather do anything than lessen God's opinion of his behavior. It is a fear that is based on respect for and love of the person one fears.

Being Blessed by the Lord

Two particular blessings were in view in the preinvasion charge. Israel was to obey (1) "that your days may be prolonged" (Deuteronomy 6:2) and (2) "that it may be well with you" (v. 3). God told Israel that if the people wanted to enjoy long, prosperous lives, His rule is simple: Obey and fear the God of heaven and you're likely to experience them.

DANGERS ANTICIPATED BY THE CHARGE

Two major dangers are anticipated by Moses' words, both of which Israel violated repeatedly.

Allowing Competition for the Heart

Deuteronomy 6:4 contains the central doctrinal statement of the Old Testament: "Hear, O Israel: The Lord our God, the Lord is one!" This is the traditional rendering of this verse, and it certainly is one way to translate it. However, it may make better sense with a slightly different rendering.

In the Hebrew text, there are only four words:

The-Lord OUR-GOD The-Lord ONE (or ONLY).

The translator has to decide where the implied verb "to be" goes. Where do you put the "is"? Many translators put it after the word "God," but I think it fits better after the first "Lord": "Hear, O Israel: The Lord is our God, the Lord only!" The grammar permits that rendering, and it suits the context better. Just to mention one point: The people to whom Moses was talking did not have any terrible difficulty with the unity of God. Would they have argued against God being one? No. Did Israel ever have any trouble conceiving of God being a Unity? No.

What the Israelites struggled with was giving their loyalty and love to the one God and excluding all others. The point is even more dramatic when you realize that the word that is used here is not the title "lord" (Hebrew *adonai*) but the personal name "Yahweh," the name

186

God chose to use when He revealed Himself to Israel. "*Yahweh* is our God," said Moses; "Yahweh *alone!*" Nobody else. Placing God on the throne is not the difficulty the people of God have always had. It is making sure that He shares it with no one.

Rarely does the person who is walking with God suddenly decide to reject Him outright. No, we gradually allow other interests to sneak in and compete for our hearts. Receiving Jesus Christ as Savior is a one-time decision. Once it's done, it never needs to be done again. Enthroning Jesus Christ, making Him supreme, and Him alone, is a moment-by-moment decision. It has to be redone every day, every hour of your life.

That is why there are such dramatic differences among people who are Christians. Take a hundred of us at random and you'll find a spectrum of behavior from the sublime to the ridiculous. Why is that? Because the fact that our names are written in heaven does not force us to love Jesus Christ supremely right now.

We should.

We have a thousand reasons to do so.

But sometimes we don't. Compromise takes place any time we act out of divided motives. Remember that the word *integrity* is based on a root that means wholeness. An integer is a whole number, not a fraction. The Christians with integrity are single-minded. They always act from the same motivation. Anything that causes us to deny our root convictions is an opportunity for compromise, a chance to disintegrate.

Waning Enthusiasm for Spiritual Things

The other danger that is anticipated by Moses' charge is apathy: "You shall love the Lord your God with all your heart, with all your soul, and with all your strength" (Deuteronomy 6:5). If you don't love the Lord with everything you've got, you will find after a while that you won't love Him at all. In the book of Second Kings, an illuminating paragraph describes the people who settled the area of Samaria after the northern kingdom was taken away to Assyria. It says, "They feared the Lord, yet served their own gods" (2 Kings 17:33). They tried to fit the true God in among the false gods. They said, in effect, "The more gods the merrier."

Their "tolerance," however, did them no credit. Whatever was real in their original fear of the Lord rapidly degenerated into theological error. By the time of the New Testament, their Samaritan religion had lost contact with the living God. Jesus said to one of them, "You [people] worship what you do not know" (John 4:22).

So what is the answer to these dangers?

THE ANSWER TO THE DANGERS

Moses gave four answers to the dangers he saw confronting them, which are essentially the dangers you and I face every day. How do you address these things?

Absorb the Precepts

We minimize our dangers by absorbing the precepts of the Word of God: "These words which I command you today shall be in your heart" (Deuteronomy 6:6). Deuteronomy is almost totally the product of a few days. Moses gathered the people who were about to go into the land and preached to them before their warfare was to begin. The book of Deuteronomy is mostly one long sermon.

That's a lot of words to put on one's heart—especially when we wonder about the value of what Moses said. Does Deuteronomy have anything to do with human experience generally? The best answer to that is to remind you that 1,400 years later Jesus Christ was compelled by the Spirit of God to go into the wilderness of Judea for forty days, and the Gospel writers tell us that while He was there He was tempted by the devil. Three times Satan placed dramatic opportunities before Him to sin. Three times the Lord Jesus quoted Scripture and told the devil to forget it. Three times He quoted from the Old Testament, and every quotation is from the book of Deuteronomy. The Lord Jesus Himself absorbed the precepts of Moses. They were on His heart. He found Deuteronomy quite relevant in the middle of one of the greatest trials of His life.

Teach the Precepts

We also minimize the dangers when we pass the truth along to a new generation: "You shall teach them diligently to your children"

(Deuteronomy 6:7). It is difficult to be neutral about matters that you have taught to others. The benefits of teaching children are not exhausted in the lives of the children. The parents are exhausted by the lives of the children, but the benefits of teaching them reflect back to the parents. When you teach your children, you are solidifying your own convictions and shaping the course of the future.

Discuss the Precepts

"You shall teach them to your children, speaking of them when you sit in your house, when you walk by the way, when you lie down, and when you rise up" (Deuteronomy 11:19). In other words, God's precepts are to be part of the common conversation of the household. Teach them formally; discuss them informally, as you go about your business.

God anticipated Israel's forgetfulness in spiritual matters.

Why is informal discussion brought into this? Because, for one thing, children can see insincerity in a minute. For another, informal discussion includes give and take. You must be able to defend what you believe if you discuss it.

Remind Yourself of the Precepts

God says to Israel in Deuteronomy 6:10–11 that He will "give you large and beautiful cities which you did not build, houses full of all good things, which you did not fill, hewn-out wells which you did not dig, vineyards and olive trees which you did not plant—when you have eaten and are full—then beware, lest you forget the Lord."

When does the danger come? "When you have eaten and are full." The greatest dangers to your spiritual life are not when you are in the battle. The greatest dangers to your spiritual life come after the battle is over and you begin to enjoy the fruits of victory.

And they are not external, but internal. "Beware, lest you forget the Lord." People do not forget the Lord in an absolute sense, of course. If you asked one of the Israelites after the Conquest, "Tell me, who is your God?" he probably could have told you God's name. However, absence from one's knowledge isn't the problem; it is absence from one's consciousness. God doesn't disappear from our memories; He disappears from our thoughts moment by moment. We have to keep reminding ourselves that all that we are and have is due to His grace and kindness. Fail to do so and you begin to drift away, a little at a time. We need reminders all around us, or drift is the natural result.

Interestingly enough, God anticipated Israel's forgetfulness in spiritual matters. Numbers 15:38–39 says, "Speak to the children of Israel: Tell them to make tassels on the corners of their garments throughout their generations, and to put a blue thread in the tassels of the corners . . . that you may look upon it and remember all the commandments of the Lord and do them." God suggested an arbitrary device almost like tying a thread around the finger. The tassels were supposed to point them back to a renewed consideration of the truth as contained in His commandments. How often were they reminded? As often as they wore clothes.

Remembering the Lord is critical.

Having a daily time in the Word is the most critically important thing you can do in your spiritual life—just opening God's book and letting His Word address you where you are. You will never get too far in a spiritual drift if you will make that one practice a regular part of your day.

The most bizarre book in the Old Testament is the book of Judges. Israel gets into more trouble spiritually and does more insane things in Judges than in any other book of Scripture. Why did it happen? Judges 8:34 says, "Thus the children of Israel did not remember the Lord their God, who had delivered them from the hands of all their enemies on every side."

They went about their business without giving Him a thought.

By contrast, the psalmist says in Psalm 119:55, "I remember Your name in the night, O Lord, and I keep Your law." The first (remembering) makes the second (keeping) possible. Let us be sure that we learn what it takes to keep Jesus Christ in our thoughts often; if we do, we will find that our lives will be enriched, and we will be people of integrity.

VICTORY

Sure I must fight if I would reign;
Increase my courage, Lord.
I'll bear the toil, endure the pain,
Supported by Thy Word.

—ISAAC WATTS

Spiritual violence forms the real business of Christian living. According to author and psychiatrist John White,

> As an image to convey the nature of Christian living, the Holy Spirit uses that of warfare. . . . The same courage, the same watchfulness, loyalty, endurance, resourcefulness, strength, skill, knowledge of the enemy, the same undying resolve to fight to the end come what may and at whatever cost must characterize Christian living as they do earthly warfare.[1]

The metaphor is an apt one, but one not widely received in the Christian community today. We like our Christian faith to be comfortable, and spiritual warfare is often no more comfortable than physical warfare. As White added, "But I am expressing it the wrong way. War is not something that illustrates aspects of Christian living. Christian living *is* war . . . the issues that hang on it make earth's most momentous questions no more than village gossip."[2]

WHAT IT TAKES TO WIN

Years ago I read an article by General Douglas MacArthur in which he described the elements necessary for military victory. I have long since forgotten the publication, but I was so impressed with what he said and with its application to the spiritual struggle that I made notes of his key points. The general listed four essential prerequisites to gaining victory in battle. First, he said, there must be adequate resources. The weapons and supplies necessary to victory must be available to the army. Second, the army that would win must be adequately trained. Third, it must have a knowledge of the enemy. Finally, it must have morale, a will to win. These four factors also lead to victory in the internal struggle for Christian character.

Resources

When it comes to self-conquest, the Christian possesses, from the moment of conversion, all the resources he needs. Peter says as much: "His divine power has given to us all things that pertain to life and godliness" (2 Peter 1:3). God's distribution of these tools for victory is not selective, but universal, because He comes personally to live within us. To say, "I can't defeat my personal sins because I don't have the ability" is to make God out to be a liar. To use Peter's terminology, "all things" means all things. The fact that we don't see our assets is meaningless. They are there. Spiritual warfare itself, after all, is not visible. Believers are able to fight and win, or God's commands that we do so become meaningless and cruel.

Training

Preparation for the conflict is available in varying degrees to today's Christian. Much can be found in print. Many individuals and churches teach the principles outlined in the preceding chapters. Unfortunately, many do not, and they pay little attention to the inner war. Anyone with a Bible and a determination to understand what God says about inner warfare can gain the insights necessary for spiritual battle. That training is best found, however, in a church family of Christians, all of whom are engaged in self-conquest. Hearing about the struggles and victories of others can prove a grand encouragement to the Christian warrior.

Knowledge of the Enemy

When it comes to self-conquest, the enemy is within. Knowing ourselves is the toughest job of all, since the heart is innately self-deceptive (see Jeremiah 17:9). We often find it comfortable to blame our own failures on others and, as a result, make little progress.

> *The most important battles are fought between the ears.*

A critical example is to be found in the relationship of what God gives us versus what He expects of us. Many a Christian has drawn wonderful encouragement from Paul's list of the fruit of the Spirit in Galatians 5:22–23, "The fruit of the Spirit is love, joy, peace, longsuffering, kindness, goodness, faithfulness, gentleness, self-control." Since fruit is the natural product of a tree, we find it easy to conclude that these virtues are items that the Spirit of God will produce in us simply because He lives within. When it doesn't happen (or happens quite slowly), we begin to wonder why. That confusion may even cause us to question whether the Spirit resides in us.

However, Galatians 5:22–23 does not exhaust what God has to say about virtues. For example, after describing how God has supplied everything necessary for godly living in 2 Peter 1:3, the author issues a command:

> *For this very reason, giving all diligence, add to your faith virtue, to virtue knowledge, to knowledge self-control, to self-control perseverance, to perseverance godliness, to godliness brotherly kindness, and to brotherly kindness*

love. For if these things are yours and abound, you will be neither barren nor unfruitful in the knowledge of our Lord Jesus Christ. (2 Peter 1:5–8)

We are to "give all diligence" (make every effort) to add certain virtues to our faith. At least two of the "fruit of the Spirit" are found here: self-control and love.

So, which is it? Are self-control and love given to us simply because the Spirit is present within, or do they become part of us through making our very best effort? The answer, of course, is both. We are to give all diligence to make self-control and love a part of our lives. Once we have done so, and those virtues become part of our character, we have the Holy Spirit to thank, for we never could have accomplished the victory without His enabling power. We must know ourselves well enough to turn away from the convenient excuses that occur so readily to us, take up the struggle, and put to death the destructive deeds of the body (see Romans 8:13). No Christian warrior gains meaningful victory who does not first become a student of his or her own heart.

Morale

Moses and Joshua spent much of their time attempting to persuade Israel that the nation could win the Promised Land. A positive, hopeful outlook must pervade spiritual warfare or it will be abandoned (as Israel eventually abandoned it). After the battle of Gibeon described in chapter 10, Joshua found the five fleeing kings of the Amorites holed up in a cave. Knowing that much fighting lay ahead,

Joshua called for all the men of Israel, and said to the captains of the men of war who went with him, "Come near, put your feet on the necks of these kings." And they drew near and put their feet on their necks. Then Joshua said to them, "Do not be afraid, nor be dismayed; be strong and of good courage, for thus the Lord will do to all your enemies against whom you fight." (Joshua 10:24–25)

As Joshua knew, the most important battles are fought between the ears. The moment a soldier begins to doubt that victory is possible, the odds of it decrease. Correspondingly, the moment he becomes convinced that he can win, he is far more likely to overcome the odds and do so. The Israelite captains received a huge morale boost as they stood that day with their feet on the necks of their enemies. They learned that they could always do more than they thought they could.

In 1863, an engineer named John Roebling came up with the idea to build a suspension bridge to tie together Brooklyn and Manhattan. People in New York knew that such a bridge was needed, but until then no one had invented a practical idea of how to do it. When Roebling told his plans, other bridge builders scoffed and assured him that his aspirations were not practical either. However, John Roebling was able to persuade his son Washington (also a civil engineer) that the project was feasible. Eventually they secured funding and completed a set of construction plans for the bridge. The Roeblings hired crews, and work began.

Only a few months into construction, however, the unthinkable happened. An accident took the life of John Roebling and injured his son so severely that he could neither move nor talk. Observers began to speculate that the project would have to be abandoned, since Washington Roebling was the only one who knew how it could be finished.

However, nothing was wrong with Washington Roebling's mind, and he was as committed as ever to the completion of the work. He discovered as he lay in bed that he could still move one finger; and he managed, with his wife's help, to invent a finger-tapping code for communicating. With only a mind and one finger in working order, Washington Roebling, over a period of thirteen years, gave the instructions needed for the Brooklyn Bridge to be finished.

God has made the Christian so that the important work of building a holy life takes place in the realm of the unseen. Though we sense our innate weakness (if we are wise), we can learn to depend on the power that God supplies in that weakness. When David confronted Goliath in the Valley of Elah (1 Samuel 17), he defeated his far more impressive enemy in part because he struck the giant in the place where battles are usually won or lost—the head. Self-conquest requires dealing with our moral lives in the realm of thought and morale. If we do that successfully, we will find that our battles are winnable.

WINNING ULTIMATE VICTORY

A large part of morale in the spiritual battle also includes seeing the personal benefits of a positive outcome to the conflict. God gave Israel one quite tangible motive as the nation sought to conquer the Land of Promise. Success would mean possession of a homeland and the partial fulfillment of the promises to Abraham, Isaac, and Jacob. A far more telling impetus to spiritual living, however, lay in the motivations of those three patriarchs. Abraham, for example, knew that the real fulfillment of God's promises lay in the heavenly city, the New Jerusalem, and so "he waited for the city which has foundations, whose builder and maker is God" (Hebrews 11:10). "Waiting" does not imply inactivity, for Abraham was nothing if not an active man. He left a sweet fragrance of the knowledge of the true God in that homeland where he owned little. He "waited" in the sense that he was able to see his aspirations in the distance and to be controlled by them.

That same was true for Isaac, who "blessed Jacob and Esau concerning things to come" (Hebrews 11:20), reminding them of the promises of God that still awaited fulfillment. Similarly, "Jacob, when he was dying, blessed each of the sons of Joseph, and worshiped" (Hebrews 11:21). The certainty of the city to come drove them to do what pleased God. This ultimate motivation still is in force when it comes to success in the spiritual conflict. As with the patriarchs, when we control our inner lives we can look forward to commendation and rewards.

These motives find confirmation in a remarkable collection of letters in the New Testament. The missives were dictated by Jesus Christ and are addressed to seven churches. The assemblies were located in what is today western Turkey, but in those days the area was known as the Roman province of Asia. The climactic expression in each letter Jesus dictated was "To him who overcomes I will give . . ." The "gifts" that follow are so remarkable that the militant believer should want to know all about "overcoming," which, as we shall see, is a military word.

For example, to the church at Laodicea Jesus wrote: "To him who overcomes I will grant to sit with Me on My throne, as I also overcame and sat down with My Father on His throne" (Revelation 3:21). To the church at Thyatira, Jesus offered an equally remarkable incentive: "He who overcomes, and keeps My works until the end, to him

I will give power over the nations—'He shall rule them with a rod of iron; they shall be dashed to pieces like the potter's vessels'—as I also have received from My Father" (Revelation 2:26–27).

The root idea in "overcoming" in these letters has to do with dealing with obstacles in order to win a prize, particularly the winning of authority in battle or gaining an award in athletics. The obstacle may be an army, another competitor, or something else. In each case, some barrier stands in the way of achievement. People who overcome are people who do battle against difficulties and win. The most prominent enemy mentioned in the letters is the world and its allurements; however, all three enemies of the believer (the world, the flesh, and the devil) appear in the letters. Ultimately, no victory over the world and the devil is possible without victory over the flesh, and Jesus Christ holds the key to that victory, as the letters to the churches note.

Each of the letters to the Asian assemblies presents a recurring pattern. The letters contain:

A description of Jesus appropriate to the needs of each church
Jesus' claim to know the works of the churches
A commendation (generally)
A rebuke (generally)
An exhortation to change
A promise to overcomers
An exhortation to take His words seriously

The common denominator of the promises to the overcomers of these letters is the honor that awaits the prevailing believer. Though much is at stake in the present age when it comes to our conduct—shame and a loss of testimony for failure, commendation and leadership for success—at the judgment seat of Christ, the Lord Jesus will publicly commend the faithful believer. "He who overcomes shall be clothed in white garments" (Revelation 3:5). The white garments in question refer not to the spotless condition of all believers in this passage, but to the public recognition of the faithful believer.

One of the common scenes of the Roman world—that is to say, the world of the New Testament—was the *triumphus,* a triumphal parade. It was every Roman general's dream to win a major victory and appear in a *triumphus*. He would be dressed in a gleaming white toga, ride through the streets of Rome in a special chariot, and come before Caesar to receive a crown emblematic of his victory. The reference to white garments fits the *triumphus* motif quite well. People who walk with Christ in white have shown themselves worthy of that intimate association (Revelation 3:4).

The letters to the churches form a loud acknowledgment to the entire world that sinning and neglectful Christians are not an unforeseen problem. The Lord Jesus is taking steps to address defection, disloyalty, and disobedience within the churches. The promises to overcomers are not veiled threats that the unfaithful believer may forfeit eternal life. They are enticing promises that leave loosely defined the details of what awaits the one who lives faithfully. The realities are so great, in fact, that words are inadequate to describe them in any case: "Eye has not seen, nor ear heard, nor have entered into the heart of man the things which God has prepared for those who love Him" (1 Corinthians 2:9).

WHAT THOSE WHO OVERCOME GAIN

The Lord Jesus will reward those who are faithful, those who overcome. Overcoming is synonymous with persistent obedience: "He who overcomes, and keeps My works until the end . . ." (Revelation 2:26). Sharing His authority during the coming kingdom of God is promised to the overcomer: "He who overcomes, and keeps My works until the end, to him I will give power over the nations—'He shall rule them with a rod of iron' . . . as I also have received from My Father" (Revelation 2:26–27).

Overcomers are also promised intimacy with Christ: "To him who overcomes I will give some of the hidden manna to eat. And I will give him a white stone, and on the stone a new name written which no one knows except him who receives it" (Revelation 2:17). Likewise: "He who overcomes, I will make him a pillar in the temple of My God, and he shall go out no more. I will write on him the name of My God and the name of the city of My God, the New Jerusalem, which comes down out of heaven from My God. And I will write on him My new name" (Revelation 3:12). Self-conquest, like all acts of faithfulness, yields the believer a treasured place among the company of those who overcome.

WHAT THOSE WHO DO NOT OVERCOME LOSE

The alternative is to relax and lose one's alertness in the inner battle. "If you do not wake up," Jesus said to the church at Sardis, "I will come like a thief, and you will not know at what time I will come to you" (Revelation 3:3 NIV). After He appears in glory, millions of somnolent Christians all over the world will feel the pain of wasted lives. Paul wrote, "There is laid up for me the crown of righteousness, which the Lord, the righteous Judge, will give to me on that Day, and not to me only but also to all who have loved His appearing" (2 Timothy 4:8). He will give that crown to all who have longed to see Him, not to all who have believed in Him.

One of those churches addressed by Jesus was in the city of Sardis, in its day one of the great cities of the world. The capital of the ancient kingdom of Lydia, in the sixth century before Christ it was ruled by a king whose name, Croesus, became a byword for immense wealth. Sardis was built on a strategically advantageous mountain outcropping. Its location made it nearly invulnerable to attack, and most invading generals were too smart even to try.

Twice in its history, however, the city had succumbed to foreign assault, first by the Persians and then by the Greeks. Sardis had been so confident it could not be attacked that it failed to guard its walls adequately. Under cover of darkness, invaders climbed the side of the ravine, entered an unwatched gate, and overthrew the city. Sardis thus was a city characterized by a complacent spirit, and the church there suffered from the same weakness. It is the least attractive of the seven churches to whom these letters are written. Our Lord finds nothing to commend about it.

Jesus wrote them, "I know your works, that you have a name that you are alive, but you are dead" (Revelation 3:1). In Sardis, the works of the church were done to impress people. They gave the church a good reputation, but the corporate life and testimony of the group was disappointing. Unfortunately there are thousands of churches like

Sardis around the world today. They give non-Christians a negative impression of Christian faith. These churches consist largely of what someone has described as "mild-mannered people, meeting in mild-mannered ways, striving to be more mild-mannered."

Victory in the conflict against all other enemies depends on our success in the inner war.

There was a time, however, when this church was alive, when it was filled with people who knew the Lord. Because they knew Him, they served the homeless and the needy of the city. That is the way they won a reputation. They appeared to be a people committed to good works, but now there was no life there. Sardis was a church that allowed a great ministry to slip away from it.

People like those in the church in Sardis, who have neglected the things that are really important, won't be happy to see Jesus at all. They are going to regret the second-rate values they have held. Their faith is effectively dead, even though it once was alive. These believers are going to be embarrassed as Christ refuses to honor them as they have refused to honor Him with their lives.

Once they are past the crisis of accountability and they find themselves in His kingdom because they believed in Him, they will be ecstatic to find themselves there. But they will not be reigning with Christ, and they will be wise enough to know that it is proper that they do not have that privilege. By contrast, the one who puts the deeds of his body to death on a daily basis will find the appearance of the Lord to be a time of joy, rest from his battles, and commendation for his victories.

And it is victories that we need, for victory in the conflict against all other enemies depends on our success in the inner war. God has told us we can; we have the equipment to do so, and all we need to do is to apply it. A holy dependence on Jesus Christ combined with an intelligent determination will help us build the kind of inner person that pleases God. Once we see the nature of the challenge and begin to delight in taking part, we will be surprised how much we can accomplish. With the Holy Spirit's power and the commitment to see the campaign through, believers can finish the internal work that God wants them to do—and, in the process, receive His approval. Nothing that this world affords can compare with that.

NOTES

INTRODUCTION: A PLEASANT SUNDAY AFTERNOON

1. "Christians Are More Likely to Experience Divorce Than Are Non-Christians," Barna Research Online, 21 December 1999. The press release may be accessed at http:// www.barna.org/cgi-bin/PagePressRelease.asp?PressReleaseID=39.
2. Doug McIntosh, *Life's Greatest Journey* (Chicago: Moody, 2000).
3. J. I. Packer, *Knowing God* (Downers Grove, Ill.: InterVarsity, 1973), 223.
4. Quoted by Robert McNally Adams as the Christian Quotation of the Day for December 9, 1999. Available by subscription online at http://gospelcom.net/cqod.

CHAPTER 1: A NEW CAMPAIGN

1. Quoted in "Bits and Pieces: Home Delivery," a free inspirational e-mail service from DailyInbox.com using quotes from *Bits & Pieces* magazine published by Economics Press. Moore's words are the daily quote from December 27, 1999. Available by subscription online at http://Your.DailyInbox.com.
2. C. S. Lewis, *Mere Christianity* (New York: Macmillan, 1963), 11.

CHAPTER 2: THE ENEMY

1. Quoted in R. Kent Hughes, *1001 Great Stories & Quotes* (Wheaton, Ill.: Tyndale, 1998), 120.
2. Ibid., 81–82.
3. Ibid., 119–120.
4. C. S. Lewis, *The Weight of Glory and Other Addresses,* rev. ed. (New York: Macmillan, 1980), 1.

CHAPTER 3: BATTLE CRY

1. C. S. Lewis, *God in the Dock: Essays on Theology and Ethics* (Grand Rapids: Eerdmans, 1970), 101.
2. I am indebted in this chapter to several lines of argument proposed by Glenn M. Miller, "Good Question," on the "Unravelling Wittgenstein's Net—A Christian Think Tank" website. His comments on the Conquest can be found at http://www.webcom.com/ctt/qamorite.html.
3. E. Stern, "War, Warfare," *Zondervan Pictorial Encyclopedia of the Bible* (Grand Rapids: Zondervan, 1975), 5:895.
4. J. Rea, "Joshua, Book of," *Zondervan Encyclopedia,* 3:707.

5. Arch D. Dickie, "City," *International Standard Bible Encyclopedia* (Grand Rapids: Eerdmans, 1979), Geoffrey W. Bromiley, ed. II:1022.

CHAPTER 4: COMMAND AUTHORITY

1. Attributed to a man who had just escaped mainland China during the Communist revolution; quoted in R. Kent Hughes, *1001 Great Stories & Quotes* (Wheaton, Ill.: Tyndale, 1998), 109.
2. Andrea Wolf, Co-Mission staff Christmas Newsletter, quoted in Hughes, *Stories & Quotes,* 393–94.
3. C. S. Lewis, *Mere Christianity* (New York: Macmillan, 1952), 87.
4. Stephen R. Covey, A. Roger Merrill, and Rebecca R. Merrill, *First Things First: To Live, To Love, To Learn, To Leave a Legacy* (New York: Simon & Schuster, 1996), 88.
5. C. S. Lewis, A Preface to "Paradise Lost," quoted in *A Mind Awake: An Anthology of C. S. Lewis* (New York: Harcourt Brace, 1968), 105.
6. Quoted in Hughes, *Stories & Quotes,* 120.

CHAPTER 5: ENCAMPMENT

1. William Shakespeare, *King Richard the Third,* 5.3.194–196.
2. Paul Deutschman, *More Stories for the Heart,* compiled by Alice Gray (Portland, Oreg.: Multnomah, 1997), 135–38.
3. Corrie ten Boom with John and Elizabeth Sherrill, *The Hiding Place* (Minneapolis: World Wide Publications, 1971), 29.
4. "Honesty and Integrity," on the Daily Help site on the World Wide Web. Available online at http://dailyhelp.com/az41.htm.

CHAPTER 6: COURAGE

1. William Shakespeare, *Macbeth,* 3.5.33.
2. C. S. Lewis, *The Screwtape Letters* (New York: Macmillan, 1942), 137–38. (Italics added.)
3. C. S. Lewis, *Surprised by Joy: The Shape of My Early Life* (New York: Harcourt Brace Jovanovich, 1955), 226.
4. Corrie ten Boom with Jamie Buckingham, *Tramp for the Lord* (Grand Rapids: Revell, 1998), 211.
5. Raymond McHenry, "Motivational Stories," a collection of illustrations on computer disk, 342. Available from the Christian Communicator's Research Service, 6130 Barrington, Beaumont, TX 77706.
6. C. S. Lewis, Letters, quoted in Clyde S. Kilby, ed., *A Mind Awake: An Anthology of C. S. Lewis* (New York: Harcourt Brace, 1980), 162.
7. The Pastor's Update (5/96) Foreign Mission Board, Southern Baptist Convention, quoted in *Leadership,* "To Illustrate," Fall, 1996. Available online at http://www.christianitytoday.com/leaders/6L4/6L4068.html.

CHAPTER 7: DEFEAT

1. Candi Cushman, "Salt or Sugar," *World,* 13 May 2000, 19.
2. Charles C. Ryrie, *So Great Salvation: What It Means to Believe in Jesus Christ* (Chicago: Moody, 1997), 13–14.

3. Eliza Edmunds Stites Hewitt, "My Faith Has Found a Resting Place."

CHAPTER 8: COMMUNICATIONS

1. Doug McIntosh, *God Up Close* (Chicago: Moody, 1998).
2. C. S. Lewis, *Mere Christianity* (New York: Macmillan, 1952), 92.
3. J. I. Packer, *Knowing God* (Downers Grove, Ill.: InterVarsity, 1973), 18–19.
4. Kris Lundgaard, *The Enemy Within* (Phillipsburg, N.J.: P&R Publishing, 1998), 47. (Italics in the original.)

CHAPTER 9: SECRETS

1. Matthew Henry, *Commentary on the Old Testament* (Albany, Ore.: AGES Software), 461. [CD-ROM].
2. The evidence for its identification with the traditional location, et-Tell, is less than compelling.

CHAPTER 10: ADVANCE

1. Aleksandr Solzhenitsyn, *The Gulag Archipelago,* quoted in "A History of Russia from Peter the Great to the Cold War," by Larry A. Taunton. Available online at http://www.altamontschool.org/ltaunton/Russia.htm.
2. Charles W. Colson, "Famous for Nothing—When Image Trumps Substance," BreakPoint Commentary for February 18, 1999. Available by e-mail subscription at http://breakpoint.org.

CHAPER 11: PRISONERS OF WAR

1. Richard Jones, *Lay My Burdens Down: A Folk History of Slavery* (Chicago: Univ. of Chicago Press, 1945), 57.

CHAPTER 12: RETREAT

1. Quoted in R. Kent Hughes, *1001 Great Stories & Quotes* (Wheaton, Ill.: Tyndale, 1998), 149.
2. Ibid., 120.

CHAPTER 13: VICTORY

1. John White, *The Fight: A Practical Handbook to Christian Living* (Wheaton, Ill.: InterVarsity, 1976), 216.
2. Ibid.

Moody Press, a ministry of Moody Bible Institute,
is designed for education, evangelization, and edification.
If we may assist you in knowing more about Christ
and the Christian life, please write us without obligation:
Moody Press, c/o MLM, Chicago, Illinois 60610.